Tejas Trikha is an Indian-born, Dubai-raised founder and writer who graduated from the University of Toronto's Rotman School of Management. While still a student, he launched CouBon, a platform that helped restaurants fill slow hours by offering deals to students, growing it to thousands of users. Alongside CouBon, he has also worked at Mubadala Capital, KPMG, and Forbes-recognized cleantech startup Xatoms. This is his first book, written to help students take action, even when they don't feel fully ready.

To my parents, without whom I would not be. To the team of CouBon, our investors, and all who stood by us through the storm. And to the quiet grace of Providence, who set me on this path and carried me through its highs and lows.

Tejas Trikha

Built Without a Budget

What I Learnt From My
Startup That Didn't Scale

AUSTIN MACAULEY PUBLISHERS
LONDON * CAMBRIDGE * NEW YORK * SHARJAH

Copyright © Tejas Trikha 2025

The right of Tejas Trikha to be identified as the author of this work has been asserted by the author in accordance with Federal Law No. (7) of the UAE, Year 2002, Concerning Copyrights and Neighbouring Rights.

All rights reserved. No part of this publication may be reproduced, stored in a retrieval system, or transmitted in any form or by any means, electronic, mechanical, photocopying, recording, or otherwise, without the prior permission of the publishers.

Any person who commits any unauthorised act in relation to this publication may be liable to legal prosecution and civil claims for damages.

ISBN – 9789948665830 – (Paperback)
ISBN – 9789948671589 – (E-Book)

Application Number: MC-02-01-8301858
Age Classification: E

The age group that matches the content of the books has been classified according to the age classification system issued by the UAE Media Council.

Printer Name: iPrint Global Ltd
Printer Address: Witchford, England

First Published 2025
AUSTIN MACAULEY PUBLISHERS FZE
Sharjah Publishing City
P.O Box [519201]
Sharjah, UAE
www.austinmacauley.ae
+971 655 95 202

"Karmanyevadhikaraste Ma Phaleshu Kadachana,
Ma Karmaphalahetur Bhur Ma Te Sangostvakarmani."
Bhagavad Gita, Chapter 2, Verse 47
"You have the right to act, but not to control the outcome.
Let not your actions be driven by the desire for results,
and do not fall into inaction out of fear of failure."

Table of Contents

Introduction Why This Book, Why Me	11
Chapter 1: Start Before You're Ready	17
Chapter 2: Building a Team with Zero Budget	25
Chapter 3: Chicken Meets Egg: Solving the Two-Sided Marketplace Paradox	34
Chapter 4: No Funding, No Problem, Until It Is	40
Chapter 5: Your Startup's Not a Startup, it's a Project Until It's Working	49
CouBon The Camera Roll Edition	59
Chapter 6: Growth Isn't Traction, Until It's Sustainable	66
Chapter 7: The System Isn't Built for Student Founders. Build Anyway	78
Chapter 8: When to Let Go (And Why That's Still Winning)	85
Conclusion What I'd Tell the 18-Year-Old Me	95

Introduction
Why This Book, Why Me

Every story has a beginning. Mine didn't start in a Silicon Valley garage with VC pitches and product demos. It began in a dorm room in Toronto, squeezed between economics lectures, cold emails, and late-night ideation sessions. But in truth, the roots of my story trace back to India, where my identity was shaped, and Dubai, where my worldview was formed.

I'm Tejas Trikha, a student, a founder, and an immigrant. Someone who built a startup that didn't scale the way I'd hoped. This is the story behind that venture, and more importantly, the lessons it left behind.

This isn't a story of billion-dollar valuations or front-page headlines. There's no viral product launch or unicorn funding round. What you'll find here instead is something far rarer: honesty. The raw, tactical, and sometimes uncomfortable truths of trying to build something from scratch, without connections, capital, or a clear playbook.

So, why me, why now, and why this book?

Why Me

I came to Canada in the fall of 2022 as an international student at the University of Toronto's Rotman School of Management, pursuing a degree in Finance and Economics. Very quickly, I realised I didn't just want to graduate with a strong GPA. I wanted to do something more. Something that mattered.

That drive came from many places. Part of it was gratitude; my family had made enormous sacrifices to get me here. Part of it was exposure; North America's hustle culture was real, visible, and often inspiring. Students were working part-time jobs to pay tuition or launching small ventures to test their ideas. And part of it was rooted in Dubai, the city I grew up in, where ambition is built into the skyline. It's a place where immigrants come to dream bigger and where every conversation carries a sense of possibility.

As someone who didn't have to worry about basic financial needs growing up, I had the privilege and responsibility to take risks. So I decided to start something. I didn't know what yet, but I knew I would.

Like many others, I was influenced by the constant flood of entrepreneurial content on Instagram and YouTube: motivational speeches, success stories, and founders stepping out of Ferraris. Eventually, I stopped watching and started building. That idea became CouBon.

CouBon was a two-sided marketplace that connected restaurants with students willing to dine during off-peak hours in exchange for discounts: a simple concept, high potential. We incorporated the business, raised external investment, partnered with over 20 restaurants, served more than 2000 students, and built a team that at one point reached 10 people. We ran it for two years, and then, in December 2024, we shut it down.

So why did CouBon close?

Primarily, two reasons.

First, our business model operated on very thin margins. We earned around $1 per transaction. To cover basic costs and eventually pay our team a fair wage, we would have needed significant scale. That kind of volume takes more time, resources, and market stability than we had.

Second, the external environment shifted. Canada was experiencing rapid food inflation, but restaurants couldn't raise prices due to stagnant household incomes. Their already-thin margins were getting thinner, and our model, which relied on offering discounts, became harder for them to justify. Many of our partner brands also mentioned concerns about upcoming U.S. tariffs, which would further pressure input costs in the industry.

In short, both our model and the market we were operating in became increasingly unfavourable. We may have had the resources to push through for another month, but certainly not another year, at least not without compromising long-term sustainability. Alongside a few operational limitations we discovered over time, closing was simply the most rational decision.

Still, what I took away was far more valuable than what I left behind. I walked away with experience, perspective, and lessons that no lecture or internship could have taught. That's why I decided to write this book.

Why Now

Not long ago, I came across a survey reporting that over 50 per cent of Gen Z aspire to become entrepreneurs at some point in their lives. Columbia Business School noted that the number of students launching startups outside the classroom had risen by nearly 30 per cent. This shift isn't limited to one country or culture. It spans cities like Toronto, Bangalore, Dubai, and New York.

And yet, most startup books are written after success, when everything is tidied up in hindsight. They reflect on challenges from the safety of a good outcome. But what about the builders still in the middle of it? The ones navigating uncertainty without a clear win in sight?

That's why now. This book is written while the experience is still fresh, while the struggles and lessons are still real. I talk not only about the strategic insights I gained, but also the emotional roller coaster that comes with being a student founder. One that includes moments of doubt, bursts of motivation, setbacks, pivots, and the search for meaning in it all.

Whether you're reading this in Dubai, Bangalore, Toronto, or New York, this journey will feel familiar. Because the challenges student founders face are more universal than we think: lack of resources, institutional apathy, the pressure to validate yourself before you're taken seriously, and the deep personal growth that happens when you're forced to figure it all out anyway. No matter where you are or how far along you may be, I hope this book serves as proof that your journey matters, even if you're still writing it.

Why This Book

After CouBon shut down, I was approached by many fellow students, most of whom I had never met. Nearly all of them were considering launching their own ventures. They asked questions that felt deeply familiar.

"How do I know if my idea is any good?"

"How do I build a team when I have no money or credibility?"

"How do I convince someone to take a chance on me?"

At first, I wondered why they were asking me. Surely, they could find all this in startup books or Y Combinator videos. But then I realised, they weren't looking for generic advice. They wanted something specific. They wanted to know what it's like to start a company as a student, with limited experience, no real network, and academic obligations pulling from the other side.

So I decided to write everything I learned, unfiltered. Two years of meetings, mistakes, wins, losses, pivots, and shutdowns. This isn't a roadmap to success, but it might be a survival guide.

I've made a conscious effort to keep this book accessible. As a student founder myself, I know how little time most of us have between classes, part-time work, and everything else life throws our way. That's why I've kept the language simple, avoided heavy technical jargon, and aimed to keep the total length manageable. My goal is for this book to be something you can actually finish, not just something you start.

What You'll Find in This Book

- Tactical breakdowns of what worked and what didn't
- Honest reflections on my own mistakes, and those I witnessed
- Raw accounts of fundraising, hiring, and pivoting under pressure
- The inner dialogue of a founder figuring things out in real time
- Snapshots of the quiet moments that no one posts about

This book is for the student founder asking Chat GPT, "How to cold email investors" at 2 a.m. It's for the builder in a small town, the international student trying to do more, or the curious mind in a city like Dubai, wondering if they're the only ones struggling to keep things afloat. And it's also for the people around us, professors, parents, and investors who support us without always seeing what it takes.

A Quick Timeline of CouBon

- **Sep 22** - Moved to Canada as an international student at the University of Toronto.
- **Oct 22** - Began initial ideation and customer discovery for CouBon.
- **Dec 22** - Incorporated the company.
- **Jan 23** - Started building the prototype app.
- **Mar 23** - Launched prototype app with four restaurant partners.
- **Jul 23** - Secured first round of seed funding from external investors.
- **Sep 23** - Orientation marketing push across university campuses.

- **Jan 24** - Relaunched app after identifying and resolving key friction points.
- **Apr 24** - Crossed 1,000 users and secured stronger brand partnerships.
- **May 24** - Reached cash flow positive status.
- **Aug 24** - Executed aggressive orientation marketing campaigns
- **Sep 24** - Grew to 2,000+ users and over 20 restaurant partners.
- **Nov 24** - Began identifying structural scalability challenges.
- **Dec 24** - Officially wound down CouBon operations.

Final Thoughts

This book isn't just about CouBon. It's about what CouBon revealed, about conviction, resilience, timing, missteps, momentum, and knowing when to build harder and when to let go. It's a reflection of the messy middle most founders live through, but rarely talk about until they're well past it. The fundraising decks, the pivots, the cold emails, the weekend breakdowns, the impossible optimism, all of it shaped me. And I suspect, in some way, it's shaping you too.

I didn't write this after a big exit or a media feature. I wrote it while the lessons were still fresh, while I could still remember the high of seeing our app hit 2,000 users, and the low of realising we wouldn't scale the way we'd hoped, while I could still feel the exhaustion from standing in the sun during back-to-back orientation fairs, and the weight of sending our final closure announcement.

But through all of it, I discovered something more valuable than a headline. I discovered what kind of builder I want to be.

Someone who leads with clarity but isn't afraid to admit confusion. Someone who knows strategy matters, but understands that culture sustains. Someone who believes in the power of ideas, but never overestimates them. And above all, someone who doesn't just build to succeed, but builds to learn.

If you're holding this book, chances are you're somewhere on the edge of your own journey. Maybe you're still toying with an idea. Maybe you're stuck in the middle of something that isn't quite working. Or maybe you're simply trying to decide whether it's time to start.

Wherever you are, you don't need to have it all figured out. I didn't. Most founders don't. What matters more is how you move forward, how you think, how you adapt, how you make decisions with imperfect information, and still show up the next day.

This book is my attempt to pass along the hard-earned insights I wish I had when I began. Not because I have all the answers, but because I now know how important the right questions can be. Questions like: What problem are you really solving? Who are you building for? What does traction *actually* mean? And how do you know when it's time to pivot, double down, or walk away?

These aren't just startup questions; they're growth questions. And they show up again and again on the journey of any builder, no matter how many companies you've run or how far you've come.

So before we get into product-market fit, funding rounds, or growth strategies, let's start at the very beginning, at the place where every venture, no matter how successful or short-lived, begins: with an idea.

Let's begin.

Chapter 1
Start Before You're Ready

There's a common misconception that you need to have everything figured out before you start a business: the perfect idea, funding, a polished pitch deck, technical co-founders, and a step-by-step roadmap. In reality, especially for student founders, that couldn't be further from the truth.

I started my startup with none of those things. No seed capital, no formal training, no industry contacts, and no grand plan. What I had was urgency, a notebook full of half-baked ideas, and a gut feeling that if I didn't start something now, I probably never would.

This chapter is about that beginning: about taking action without complete clarity, launching with more instinct than information, and realising that starting before you feel "ready" is often the only way anything gets built at all.

The Spark

It began with a simple observation. As a new student in Toronto trying to stretch every dollar, I noticed restaurants were either packed or completely empty, rarely anything in between. At the same time, students constantly complained about how expensive eating out had become, not just for the food, but for the experience of going out with friends. Clearly, there was inefficiency waiting to be addressed.

Coming from Dubai, a city where luxury and value co-exist, and having roots in India, where frugality is a cultural reflex, I naturally saw the gap. I had grown up watching price-conscious consumers hunt for the best deals, and high-end restaurants offer steep weekday discounts to draw in traffic. That lens made it easy to recognise that what looked like randomness in Toronto's restaurant traffic was actually untapped capacity. Most people around me saw a quiet restaurant and walked past. I saw an underutilised asset waiting to be optimised.

I started paying closer attention to the patterns. Bubble tea places would be overflowing at 4 p.m. but completely dead by 7. Some mid-tier restaurants had elaborate lunch deals but struggled to attract even five tables on weekday evenings. I even chatted with some servers off the record who said their slow shifts were the worst because they felt unproductive and anxious about tips. From a student lens, this created an interesting symmetry: students had time and were price-sensitive; restaurants had empty tables and couldn't afford to be. There was clearly a market inefficiency; what was missing was the bridge. Our startup aimed to become that.

This wasn't the first idea I explored. My early notebook was filled with rough concepts, a part-time job matcher for students, a peer-to-peer delivery app where students could bring groceries or food for others on their route, and even a campus-only dating platform. The last one, amusingly, gained traction among other student founders but failed to scale, likely due to the steep challenge of achieving network effects in an already crowded space. Some ideas were too niche, others hard to monetise, and most didn't pass the simple test: *Would I actually use this?* What struck me about the dining concept was its universality. The problem was obvious, the audience clear, and the path to building felt possible.

I remembered a discount app from Dubai that gave users access to premium restaurant deals. What if we could bring a localised, student-focused version of that to Toronto? Charging students wasn't an option; most were already price-sensitive. But what if we monetised from the restaurant side?

The question then became: why would restaurants pay us? Toronto's food scene is fragmented, with many restaurants owned by immigrant families lacking big marketing budgets. Their advertising often consisted of sidewalk chalkboards or static posters with time-based discounts, methods that rely on foot traffic and familiarity. In a competitive, digitally driven world, these approaches weren't working.

Meanwhile, rising overheads, rent, utilities, and labour meant that idle capacity during off-peak hours was burning cash. If we could reliably drive footfall during these low-demand windows, restaurants would have reason to pay. On the other side, students, known for flexible schedules, might be more than willing to eat lunch at 3 p.m. if it meant saving a few bucks.

Building From Scraps

I spent hours researching whether anything like this already existed. Most food apps in Canada were focused on takeout or general coupons. But dine-in, with its social, experiential value, was different, especially for students.

To validate the idea, I started asking around. Friends and classmates liked it. Restaurant managers were intrigued. I didn't have a formal survey or a fancy dashboard. I had word-of-mouth validation and a growing sense that I needed to build.

One of my earliest steps was finding a name. I wasn't thinking about pitch decks or tech stacks yet; I just wanted something that captured the spirit of the idea. Our first attempt was "Fuzon," a mashup of "fun" and "zone," meant to evoke a place where students could enjoy life affordably. But it was too vague, too forgettable. "Coupon" was the obvious fallback, but it was far too generic and unavailable. Then came "CouBon", a blend that kept the coupon reference while adding a clever twist: *bon*, the French word for "good." Given Canada's bilingualism, it felt relevant, catchy, and student-friendly. That name gave the idea identity.

That one decision, picking a name, made the abstract feel tangible. Suddenly, it wasn't just "my app idea." It was CouBon. Something I could pitch, brand, and bring others into. That psychological shift made it easier to talk to people, recruit support, and even envision a future for the product. A name gives an idea a body; it helps others believe it exists, even before it really does.

For founders in North America, I'd recommend running a NUANS report, a paid but essential search tool that checks for existing trademarks and business names. It's often required for incorporation and can save you legal headaches down the road.

With the name in place, we needed a logo and colour scheme. My co-founder, Rick, helped set up a call with a graphic designer from Japan, who kindly offered to help for free. Sometimes, simply showing up and asking for help, even from unlikely places, can work in your favour. After several rounds of ideas, we landed on a pink-and-white palette that felt vibrant, youthful, and energetic. The logo was a bold "C" with a "B" tucked beneath it, simple, distinct, and flexible. It wasn't perfect, but it gave us a sense of legitimacy. And in the early days, those small wins matter. They keep morale high when nothing feels real, yet sometimes, that momentum is what keeps you going.

Looking back, some things I did early on were strategic. Others were shortsighted. Here's what worked, and what I would change.

Start Before You're Ready

This mindset saved me from analysis paralysis. Too many student founders sit on their ideas, waiting for everything to align. But, as Mark Zuckerberg said, *"Ideas don't come out fully formed. They only become clear as you work on them. You just have to get started."*

Had I waited for the perfect moment, CouBon never would have existed. Many student founders think they'll launch once they gain work experience or raise funds. But real life doesn't get easier. The older you get, the more complex your responsibilities become, from mortgages and family to career stability. The earlier you start, the more space you have to stumble, learn, and adapt.

In my case, launching CouBon before I felt ready meant learning on the go, from figuring out legal incorporation to pitching restaurants and building an early team. Each step revealed new gaps I hadn't anticipated, but it also pushed me to move faster, ask better questions, and grow into the role rather than wait to feel qualified for it.

I remember walking into my first restaurant pitch with nothing but enthusiasm and a Canva slide. I was so confident the owner would be sold in minutes. Instead, he asked basic operational questions I hadn't even considered: How will reservations be tracked? Will staff be trained? What's the refund process if a student misuses the deal? I had no answers. But rather than letting that demoralise me, I went back, asked more questions, revised my pitch, and learned fast. That was the first time I realised that launching doesn't just expose gaps, it gives you the urgency to close them.

Share Your Idea

One trap first-time founders fall into is secrecy. Afraid their idea will be stolen, they operate in isolation. I didn't, and that made all the difference. As Michael Seibel of Y Combinator said, *Ideas are worthless. Execution is everything.*

Look at electric cars. GM and Ford attempted EVs years before Tesla. What Tesla got right wasn't the idea; it was the execution. Talking about your idea early helps you refine it, pressure-test it, and attract collaborators who can elevate it.

With CouBon, I openly discussed the concept with peers, mentors, and even potential users. These conversations surfaced perspectives I hadn't considered, helped me tweak features, and in one case, even led to a key partnership. That openness became a real asset.

That said, not all feedback is useful. People will offer conflicting advice with equal conviction. It was mindboggling to have one person call CouBon a "game-changer" and another, on the same day, say it would never work. The trick is to stop focusing on whether people think the idea is good or bad, and instead zero in on what specific needs or behaviours it does or doesn't address. That's where the real insights lie.

Mistakes I Made (So You Don't Have To)

The Availability Bias:

Most of my early validation came from people in my immediate network, classmates, friends, and people with similar backgrounds. Naturally, they liked the idea. But when we launched, adoption was slower than expected. Similarly, restaurant managers were supportive, but when I pitched owners, many hesitated. Their concerns weren't always rational, ranging from discomfort with unfamiliar tech to scepticism about discounts or just plain inertia. I should have cast a wider net much earlier.

Had I done so, I would've surfaced some key concerns in time to address them before launch. For instance, our initial product required restaurant staff to enter a redemption code directly into the customer's phone. In theory, it was efficient. In practice, it felt invasive and was a time drain for busy staff. We eventually reworked it, but the delay cost us goodwill and momentum. A broader range of early feedback could have saved us from that detour.

Looking back, this wasn't just a strategic misstep; it shook my confidence. I had convinced myself that once we launched, users would just show up. When they didn't, I began questioning the entire idea. It took several weeks of painful recalibration to realise that slow adoption didn't mean rejection; it meant I had overlooked some key friction points. That distinction saved me from quitting too early.

Vague Validation Questions:

"Would you use this app?" is a polite trap. People often say yes just to be agreeable. Instead, I should have asked questions rooted in real behaviour:

- When was the last time you skipped eating out because of the price?
- How do you currently find discounts?
- Would you shift your meal time for a better deal?

Specific questions reveal pain points, while vague ones get you feel-good lies.

Most startup ideas do offer some benefit, but the key question is whether that benefit outweighs the cost, monetary or otherwise, of using the product. In CouBon's case, it wasn't just about saving money; it was also about convincing students to try unfamiliar restaurants or go out of their way in the cold for a small discount. Behavioural insights like these are crucial not only for refining your minimum viable product (beta) but also when selecting your target audience later on.

For instance, a student who regularly cooks to avoid eating out probably won't change their habits for a minor deal. But someone who already eats out once a week might be nudged into a second outing if the value proposition feels worthwhile. These distinctions, uncovered through smarter questioning, can guide both product development and marketing strategy.

Assuming Rationality:

Rationality doesn't always hold. This was one of my key miscalculations. On paper, a 20% discount sounds like a no-brainer. Who wouldn't want to save money on a meal? But in practice, it translated to around $3 off a $15 lunch. When that meant walking ten minutes out of your way in sub-zero temperatures, many students simply passed. The math worked, the logic checked out, but the behaviour didn't follow.

This was an early lesson in the difference between economic incentives and human behaviour. We often assume users will make choices like rational agents, weighing costs and benefits with perfect clarity. In reality, people factor in convenience, comfort, emotion, and habit. A small deal isn't compelling if the friction to redeem it is even slightly annoying.

To avoid falling into this trap, founders must go beyond theoretical validation. Surveys and spreadsheets are helpful, but insufficient. Run pilots. Observe real behaviour. If your concept hinges on users making a specific choice, changing their routine, timing, or platform, test that assumption before scaling. What people say they'll do and what they actually do are rarely the same.

In CouBon's case, we could have run quick trials, say, handing out physical coupons at unusual hours and seeing how many were actually redeemed. That low-tech test alone might've saved us weeks of overbuilding a feature that relied on unrealistic user behaviour. Rationality may drive your model, but irrationality will shape your user experience. Learn to anticipate both.

The Three Questions

At nearly every pitch event or venture capital panel I attended, the same three questions came up: Why this? Why you? Why now?

For CouBon, the first two were easy to answer. "Why this?", because there wasn't a single platform where restaurants could dynamically adjust prices throughout the day to increase footfall, especially among students. Dine-in traffic during off-peak hours was a genuine pain point, and no one was addressing it in a targeted way.

"Why you?" because I was living the problem. As a student myself, I understood the behaviours, schedules, and motivations of our core user base. I also had access to university channels that gave us organic visibility and early traction.

But "Why now?", that one was harder to justify. I loosely pointed to the post-COVID inflationary environment and the looming recession, arguing that rising price sensitivity made timing ideal. But in truth, no technological or behavioural inflection point made 2023 the only time this could be built.

Compare that with Uber, which launched just as smartphones, GPS accuracy, and mobile payments converged to make e-hailing possible. Or Airbnb, which came to life in the aftermath of the 2008 recession, as people were more willing to monetise their homes and trust strangers online, supported by the rise of review systems and digital infrastructure.

If your idea could have been launched three years earlier but wasn't, that's worth investigating. Often, there's a hidden reason, lack of infrastructure, market readiness, or just user behaviour, that prevented its success until now. Ignoring that can leave you solving the right problem, but at the wrong time.

Final Thoughts

One of the most persistent myths in entrepreneurship is that clarity is a starting condition. Before you take a step, you need a plan, a model, and a pitch deck that connects every dot. In truth, clarity is something you earn through action, through stumbles, and through learning as you go. CouBon didn't begin with a grand vision or a polished roadmap. It began with a question that wouldn't leave me alone and a quiet discomfort with the way things were.

And that was enough, at least to start.

The name, the brand, the strategy, the structure, all of it came later, shaped by small wins and large corrections. That's the part people underestimate: most of what makes a startup "real" doesn't exist until you build it. And most of what makes a founder grow doesn't come from planning; it comes from doing.

But starting, while powerful, is also isolating. In the beginning, all you have is an idea in your head and a conviction in your gut. No users to validate it, no partners to share it with, no team to share the weight. It's easy to forget how heavy it all feels when it's just you carrying the uncertainty. The excitement fades quickly when there's no one to echo it back.

That's when the loneliness creeps in. Not the kind that comes from being physically alone, but the kind that comes from building something no one else can fully see yet. It's why those first people you bring on matter so much, not just for what they build, but for what they believe. Before the product is working, before the pitch is refined, before a single customer signs up, you need people who are in, not because it's obvious, but because it's worth believing in.

Finding those people, convincing them to join you, and leading them without authority or money, those are tests of character, not just competence. And they shape your company in ways that spreadsheets never can. Those early hires, those shared coffee-fuelled brainstorms, those nights spent working on a logo no one will see for months, they form the culture long before you have an HR policy.

What I learned, often the hard way, is that the courage to begin must be matched by the humility to build with others. You can't scale a vision alone, and even the most determined founder needs others to make the impossible feel a little more possible.

The idea may get you started, but the team is what keeps you moving.

Chapter 2
Building a Team with Zero Budget

You don't need a sleek office, venture capital, or a ping-pong table to build an early-stage team that lasts. What you do need is belief, both yours and theirs.

When CouBon was nothing more than an idea, I knew I couldn't build it alone. I wasn't a developer, nor did I have formal training in operations, branding, or law. But I had conviction, a willingness to lead from the front, and a set of ambitious classmates willing to take a chance on something unproven.

The Real First Step

The journey didn't begin with a pitch deck or a prototype; it began with a series of late-night conversations. A friend and I started spending weekends brainstorming what CouBon could be. These weren't polished strategic meetings, but chaotic scribble sessions about student life, restaurant footfall patterns, and what might actually get someone to use our app.

In parallel, I began drafting a business plan. Not to show investors, but for internal clarity. The process of writing it forced us to think about financial viability, monetisation strategies, and user behaviour. It wasn't glamorous, but it was necessary. It took nearly six weeks, but it left me with a much deeper clarity of what I was building, something paramount to have before we went recruiting others to join the team.

Finding the Right Builder

While our strategy sharpened, we had no way to build anything, for neither my friend nor I possessed the expertise to code our app. That changed one night when a student barged into my friend's dorm room while we were brainstorming, to show off a Chrome extension he had developed. His enthusiasm was infectious. As he animatedly explained how it saved browser energy, I recognised someone with rare technical conviction and the ability to follow through. In that moment, I knew I was speaking to one of those quietly brilliant minds who don't just think, they build. So when it came time to find a technical powerhouse to bring our product to life, Rick Huang was the first and only person who came to mind.

When I pitched CouBon to Rick, he paused. Then he said, "I'll join you, but only if you promise not to give up like most people do." That moment marked a turning point; we now had our CTO. As Rick and I began shaping how we wanted the app to look and feel, we were well aware of the uphill road ahead. Neither of us had ever built or launched an app before, and navigating the structure, design, and approval process for the App and Play Stores was uncharted territory. More pressing still, we needed restaurants to actually list on the platform; without them, there was no product to offer.

But despite the challenges, we had something crucial: momentum and belief. And for a student startup, that's a powerful place to begin.

Cracks, Fatigue, and Incorporation

Compounding the pressure of building the app was the fact that the rest of the team had fallen quiet. My original brainstorming partner and our tentative CFO had gone radio silent. From drafting the business plan and exploring the legal structure to coordinating the logo design, I was doing it all. It wasn't the volume of work that weighed on me; it was the growing sense of isolation.

To break the inertia, I made a pivotal decision: to incorporate the company. Not just as a legal necessity, but as a morale catalyst. Something tangible that gave CouBon form, and signalled to others, and to myself, that this was real.

But incorporation in North America came at a cost. And I had made a quiet promise to myself early on, I wouldn't lean on family money or accept handouts just because I was someone's child or relative. I wanted CouBon to be taken seriously, starting with how it was funded. So I approached two trusted friends, formalised loan agreements with repayment timelines and clearly defined equity terms, and secured our first capital, $4,000 in total.

On December 28th, 2022, CouBon was officially incorporated. To this day, I remain deeply grateful to Ethan and Daniel. They didn't invest in a product. They invested in belief. That capital gave us just enough fuel to start, to register accounts, set up our basic infrastructure, and begin work on our MVP.

Making It Tangible

Once CouBon was officially incorporated, things began to move with greater purpose. One of our early wins came from an unlikely connection, a graphic designer based in Japan, with whom Rick had previously worked. Despite the time zones and lack of budget, she agreed to help us for free, moved by the spirit of the project. Together, we finalised a logo that felt young and unapologetically bold, a clean white "C" and "B" set against a vivid gradient pink backdrop. The colour wasn't just aesthetic. It signalled energy, optimism, and a student-friendly vibe, something that would stand out on a cluttered phone screen.

While the visual identity took shape, Rick threw himself into the back-end development. With no prior experience in app development, we had to learn on the go, reading developer documentation, navigating the technical prerequisites of the App and Play Stores, and figuring out what could realistically be built with our constraints. But by January 2023, Rick had something to show: our first working beta. It was simple, bare-bones even, but it functioned, and in those early days, that was enough.

For the first time, CouBon felt real not just to us, but to others. We had something to demonstrate to potential restaurant partners, something tangible to show classmates we were trying to recruit, and something we could point to when others dismissed the idea as just another student project. When people can see and touch what you're building, belief follows. And belief is a powerful currency, especially when you're still running on almost nothing else.

Sales, Exits, and The Early Core

With a working beta in hand, the next hurdle was onboarding restaurants, the lifeblood of our platform. Around this time, we brought on two student sales associates to help me conduct door-to-door outreach across the city. We offered a small commission per onboarded restaurant, but the job was anything but easy. Our app wasn't yet live, and all we had to present was a rough beta build and a few printed screenshots clipped to a sheet of paper. To most restaurant owners, we must've looked like exactly what we were: a group of wide-eyed university students pitching a half-formed idea in the dead of the Canadian winter.

We visited well over a hundred restaurants, trudging through snow, facing repeated rejections, and often being politely (or not-so-politely) shown the door. Still, we kept going. And then, finally, a breakthrough, a small eatery tucked away in a narrow alley of downtown Toronto agreed to give us a shot. It wasn't fancy, but it was real. It was our first customer.

I still remember the moment I tried to pay Ali Tahir, the sales associate who had brought the restaurant on board. At the time, the funds we'd raised through our initial loan were already thinning out. When I handed him the agreed-upon $25 commission, he surprised me. "Give it to me once CouBon turns a profit," he said, smiling. It was a small gesture, but it hit hard. In a world where everything feels transactional, here was someone who genuinely believed in the long game.

That moment solidified something. I asked Ali to take on a broader role, to lead restaurant partnerships as our de facto COO. He agreed and became the third pillar of our fledgling team, alongside Rick and me.

Meanwhile, I was still searching for a new CFO. Our initial one had quietly exited, along with my original brainstorming partner, once the reality of the workload set in. For a while, it was just the three of us: Rick, Ali, and I, building in silence, sustained more by conviction than certainty.

Eventually, we brought in a friend to help shape and refine our financial model, stepping in as our new CFO. Slowly, our early team began to take shape, not built on resumes or credentials, but on belief, shared struggle, and quiet resilience.

Key Takeaways

That early phase, building with a small, rotating cast of contributors, taught me more about people than any classroom ever could. With each new teammate, each departure, and each quiet breakthrough, I started to recognise patterns. I began to understand the types of people who gravitate towards university startups, what motivates them, and the subtle red flags that hint at future disengagement. These weren't just abstract observations; they were hard-earned lessons that shaped how I approached team building going forward. I've distilled some of those insights below.

The Three Types of Student Joiners

Over time, I identified three recurring types of people who join university startups:

1. **The Stepping-Stoners.** These individuals treat startups as temporary stepping stones to land bigger corporate internships and jobs. While they're often capable and can contribute meaningfully in the short term, they're not the people you want in your core team. The startup will never be their first priority, and when you're pulling long hours and struggling to stay motivated, that lack of alignment can drag the entire team down.
2. **The Optimists.** They genuinely believe they want to be part of a startup, but they underestimate the grind. These are the ones who start strong, only to fade when the long hours, uncertainty, and ambiguity kick in. They don't mean to let you down; in fact, they're often just as surprised by their own burnout. My initial brainstorming partner fell into this category. He had the heart, but not the stamina. As a founder, it's important to spot these people early and have a respectful, honest conversation when it's time to part ways.
3. **The Builders.** Rare, but essential. These are the ones who don't need hand-holding. They self-start, take initiative, and thrive in messy, ambiguous environments. They believe in the mission and operate with a sense of ownership, even without pay or external validation. Rick and Ali were part of this small but vital group. If you're lucky enough to find one, do everything you can to keep them: they are the backbone of your early-stage company.

How to Motivate People Without Money

Understanding who is on your team is only half the equation; the other half is learning how to keep them engaged when you can't offer traditional incentives. In the absence of salaries or perks, motivation must be cultivated deliberately. Over time, I discovered three powerful ways to inspire commitment and performance in a resource-constrained startup environment.

1. **Equity with structure.** Equity is the default currency of early-stage startups, but it only works if handled properly. Giving away shares too

loosely leads to dead equity, where people who are no longer involved still hold ownership. That not only frustrates future teammates, it also deters investors who scrutinise cap tables. The solution is a clear vesting schedule, typically over four years with a one-year cliff, which ensures people earn their stake gradually. This wasn't just theoretical for us. From day one, I created formal agreements that outlined exactly how equity would be distributed and under what conditions. I used tools like LawDepot to draft clear contracts, showing we were operating with professionalism and intention.

2. **Appeal to intrinsic motivators.** When money isn't on the table, purpose has to be. You need to connect with what drives people internally, whether it's a desire to build something meaningful, gain entrepreneurial experience, or prepare for launching their own venture. Early on, I had one-on-one conversations with each teammate about their long-term goals. I wanted to understand what they were aiming for so I could show them how CouBon could help get them there. When people see your venture as aligned with their future ambitions, they become far more invested in the mission.

3. **Model relentless drive.** Above all, motivation is contagious. As the founder, your energy sets the tone. I had a simple rule: if someone else worked five hours, I'd work fifteen. I made myself available for calls at midnight, stayed responsive even during exams, and carried the weight when others couldn't. I didn't do this to impress anyone; I did it because I believed in what we were building. But that belief had ripple effects. When your team sees you giving your all, it becomes hard not to match that energy. Consistency and passion from the top create the cultural glue that holds everything together.

Additional Lessons from the Trenches

Motivation lays the foundation, but structure keeps the house standing. Over the course of CouBon's early days, I learned several hard-won lessons about building a strong team not from textbooks or entrepreneurship podcasts, but through trial and error, and countless late-night conversations. These are the insights I'd share with any student founder about how to lead, organise, and evolve your startup team from zero.

- **Don't give out titles unless there's a need.** In our earliest days, we didn't need a CFO, and yet we had one. As a finance student, I could handle the financial modelling and bookkeeping myself. But giving someone a big title too early only creates false expectations and misalignment. It's tempting to stack your LinkedIn page with "C-suite" teammates, but premature titles often lead to unnecessary churn and confusion about roles.
- **Incorporation creates both pressure and credibility.** The day we became a legal entity, something shifted. Suddenly, CouBon wasn't just a fun side project; it was a registered business with a name, structure, and responsibilities. Incorporation gave our team something tangible to rally around. Founders don't get the dopamine hit of a bi-weekly paycheck, so it's crucial to create small wins. Moments like incorporating, choosing a logo, or getting your first download can serve as psychological fuel to keep the team going.
- **Document everything.** Whether it's equity splits, reimbursement terms, or partnership roles, write it down. In the early stages, it's easy to rely on goodwill and verbal agreements, but informality is a ticking time bomb. Formal documentation doesn't just reduce future conflict; it also makes your startup look far more legitimate to future investors, advisors, and hires.
- **Smaller, committed teams beat bloated, disengaged ones.** It's far better to build with three motivated people than to manage ten who are half in. Early-stage startups thrive on belief, not headcount. When resources are limited and stakes are high, alignment matters more than sheer numbers. A smaller team, when fully bought in, can often move faster, communicate better, and adapt quicker than a larger, scattered one.
- **Choose People Who Can Handle Pressure.** In a student startup, time is your most limited resource. That's why I leaned towards teammates who were already performing well academically. It wasn't about grades, but grit. If someone couldn't manage deadlines and pressure in the classroom, they usually cracked under the faster, messier chaos of a startup. Academic success isn't a perfect filter, but in a university setting, it's often the best early signal of someone's discipline and

follow-through. Pick people who've shown they can handle the load, because startup pressure doesn't get lighter.

- **Equity should be earned, not gifted.** Don't give shares just to entice someone to join. Use cliffs and vesting schedules to ensure equity is tied to contribution over time. And if someone leaves early, be ready to revoke what hasn't been earned. Investors pay close attention to cap tables; widely distributed, unearned equity is a red flag that can kill deals before they start.
- **Early churn isn't a crisis; it's a filter.** In CouBon's two-year journey, we had many entries and exits. Every time a core team member left, it stung. It felt personal. But in hindsight, nearly every departure made room for someone better suited to the demands of the moment. Losing a teammate may feel like a setback, but it's often a necessary step in refining your team to match the company's evolving needs.

Final Thoughts

One of the hardest truths about building anything from scratch, especially as a student founder, is that the early stages are less about execution and more about endurance. Yes, you need to think. Yes, you need to strategise. But mostly, you need to hold the line long enough to turn belief into momentum. And you can't do that alone.

When CouBon started, I thought the first real challenge would be building the product. But I quickly realised the harder part was building the team. Not the kind of team you read about in headlines or investor updates, but the kind that shows up when nothing is working yet. The kind that sticks around not because of perks or paychecks, but because something in them resonates with what you're trying to do.

Bringing in those people required a different kind of leadership, one that didn't rely on authority, experience, or even resources. I had to lead with conviction, clarity of purpose, and a willingness to go first. I learned that people don't follow because of what you've already built; they follow because of what you're willing to build in front of them, from scratch, with no guarantees. And if you're asking others to believe in something unproven, you'd better believe in it twice as hard.

But belief alone isn't enough. I had to learn how to structure it, how to document equity, how to think about incorporation, how to signal that we weren't just another student project floating on enthusiasm. We had to become real. And really, in the startup world, it's often less about revenue and more about rhythm: Do you show up when it's hard? Do you respond when the stakes feel small? Do you build when no one's watching?

And yet, even as the company became "real" on paper, with a logo, a legal status, and a beta build, there was still the emotional weight of seeing people leave. Of teammates who disappeared quietly. Of trying to explain why someone who once brainstormed beside you is no longer around. These moments weren't just logistical setbacks; they were emotional fractures. Because when you're building in the dark, every person who leaves takes a little bit of light with them.

But then, someone else steps in. Someone who isn't deterred by the lack of polish or profit. Someone who wants to build, not just benefit. And slowly, the momentum returns. Those quiet moments of shared grind, the first user sign-up, the first restaurant onboarded, the first time someone says *"this is actually useful"*, they start to stack up. And each one builds trust not just in the product, but in each other.

Looking back, I don't remember the exact lines of code or the fonts we debated for our branding. I remember the late nights when Rick and I tried to figure out the Play Store approval forms. I remember Ali refusing his first commission because he believed we'd make it eventually. I remember the conversations where I asked someone to bet their limited time on something that wasn't real yet, and they said yes.

These moments didn't just shape CouBon. They shaped me. They showed me that while founders often get the spotlight, it's the team that earns the story.

And once we had that team: small, gritty, and deeply invested, we had permission to take the next step: to take what we'd built behind the scenes, and finally bring it to the world.

Chapter 3
Chicken Meets Egg: Solving the Two-Sided Marketplace Paradox

By early 2023, we had the essentials in place: a name that people would remember, a basic prototype app, and a small, committed team. But now came the real test: proving that CouBon could survive outside the comfort of pitch decks, brainstorming sessions, and group chats.

The challenge was straightforward to describe but brutal to solve: no student would download an app with no restaurants, and no restaurant wanted to join a platform with no users. Welcome to the classic two-sided marketplace paradox, a riddle that has frustrated startups from Airbnb to Uber, and now, CouBon.

Starting With Supply: Getting Restaurants Onboard

We decided to focus on onboarding restaurants first. Without them, there was nothing to offer users. Our first restaurant came through Ali, but the pace didn't pick up quickly after that. Day after day, we walked through the snow, knocking on doors with nothing but printouts of our beta app, trying to look more legitimate than we felt.

Restaurant owners were rarely present. Employees, often cautious or indifferent, refused to share contact details. All we'd get was a generic email, which never yielded responses. So we kept returning, timing our visits around slow hours and hoping to find the decision-maker.

Even when we did catch the owner, scepticism was high. Some said they'd think about it, others flatly refused, and a few agreed with conditions, offering discounts as small as five or ten per cent. Still, we celebrated every small win.

One yes out of fifty conversations meant progress. By March, we had four restaurants on board, modest but real.

I still remember when I began visiting certain restaurants so frequently that the staff started to recognise me, offer me water, and sometimes even small tasters. It was their way of acknowledging the effort. In a sea of no's, these tiny moments made a difference.

Selling Through Cultural and Generational Barriers

This early hustle was a crash course in real-world sales. I realised quickly that persuasion wasn't just about value propositions: it was about relationships.

Cultural factors played a major role. Some owners, especially from traditional backgrounds, were uncomfortable with the idea of offering discounts. One restaurant owner told me, *"Guests are like gods. We host them with honour. Discounts cheapen that."*

Others were open-minded but confused. The business model, the tech platform, the revenue impact, it all felt too new. Generational differences were stark, too. Younger, second-generation owners were more likely to embrace the idea. Older ones saw us as students playing pretend.

To bridge the gap, I tapped into shared values and personalisation. For Asian owners, I used our common culture to build trust, showing up in person, remembering birthdays, and treating every conversation with deep respect. I once took an hour-long bus ride early on a Sunday morning just to wish a partnered restaurant owner a happy birthday in person. For Western owners, I tapped into the common experience of hustling, which they fondly remembered doing during their college days

In another case, when an elderly owner experienced technical difficulties onboarding to CouBon, I visited his shop to assist personally, only to realise he had entered the wrong email. Still, that effort to show up built credibility. With every visit, it became less about persuasion and more about partnership.

When an owner was too senior or traditional, I would try to approach their children, often more tech-savvy and open to experimentation. It wasn't manipulation, it was alignment. Once they believed in us, convincing the rest of the team became easier.

The App Store Battle

With a few restaurants on board, the next mountain loomed: publishing on the App Store and Play Store. For the uninitiated, this process is rigorous. You need developer accounts, proper documentation, working code, and legal disclaimers. Then comes the waiting game, and usually, rejection.

Our app was rejected three times. Each time, vague feedback left us guessing. I'll never forget the night Rick knocked on my dorm room door, eyes filled with frustration. Rejection number three had come in. He broke down, overwhelmed by the setbacks. I didn't. I put on a brave face, told him this was part of the journey, and promised we'd push through.

In reality, I was terrified. Our initial funds were almost gone. We had little left to fall back on. But I knew I couldn't let the team feel that fear. That night, I learned a foundational lesson in leadership: never transmit panic. Absorb it.

And I carried that lesson with me for the rest of CouBon's journey. Whether a restaurant dropped us at the last minute, a developer missed a deadline, or we faced cash flow issues, I learned to communicate optimism while privately planning for the worst. This wasn't about deception; it was about anchoring the team during instability. That mindset of being the emotional thermostat allowed CouBon to maintain momentum during its most uncertain periods.

That week, Rick went back to debugging and revising, trying to guess what might be going wrong with our submission. We reviewed our onboarding process, rewrote the App Store listing, cleaned up our privacy terms, and tweaked the UI. Each fix was a shot in the dark, but each attempt taught us more about the rigour of launching in a formal digital space.

The Breakthrough

In late April, we got the email we had been waiting for. CouBon was officially live on the App and the Play Store.

It was a quiet celebration, as we had under $500 left in our bank account. But we had crossed a major milestone. In under six months, we had gone from idea to implementation. A real app. A real team. Real restaurants. And a mission that was finally taking shape in the real world.

I remember just staring at the CouBon icon on my phone, almost in disbelief. The same idea that started as a scribble in my notes was now searchable and downloadable by anyone in the world.

Key Takeaways: Building the Two-Sided Engine

- **Start where the friction is lowest.**
  For CouBon, that meant going after restaurants first. While students wouldn't download an empty app, restaurants could be persuaded on the promise of future demand. Supply had to precede demand, even if it meant walking door-to-door in the dead of winter with nothing more than a basic prototype and belief. Our thinking was simple: a student might download the app once there's something to gain, but a restaurant needs to be convinced of a future pipeline, and that's a harder, slower sell. By tackling that first, we were setting the foundation.

- **Relationships beat resumes and rehearsed pitches.**
  In our earliest meetings, it became clear that logic alone wouldn't win over restaurant owners. Cultural values, generational gaps, and emotional instincts all shaped how people responded. For example, some owners were philosophically opposed to discounts, equating them with lowered dignity. Others distrusted tech platforms or didn't want to be the "first mover." In those moments, professionalism wasn't enough; what mattered was sincerity. I learned to build familiarity: remembering birthdays, helping troubleshoot backend issues in person, commuting long distances just to show up. When credibility is scarce, trust becomes your currency.

- **Rejection is feedback in disguise.**
  The App Store rejected us three times. Dozens of restaurant owners brushed us off. But rejection rarely means the door is locked forever. At CouBon, we learned to treat every "no" as a "not yet", a signal to return with better answers. When restaurants gave specific concerns about revenue dilution, tech confusion, or student reliability, we documented them, refined our pitch, and returned weeks later with tailored solutions. The difference that the follow-up made was remarkable. People respected the grit and, more often than not, changed their tune.

- **Track your progress with precision.**
  We maintained a detailed spreadsheet logging every restaurant we approached, who visited when, what was discussed, and the current

status. This prevented duplicate outreach, helped us follow up more strategically, and maintained professionalism across our small but growing team.

- **As the founder, your tone becomes your team's temperature.**
  One of the most important lessons I learned was this: never transmit panic. The night Rick broke down after our third app rejection, I stayed calm, reassuring him even though I myself was quietly spiralling. That instinct to protect morale, to absorb chaos and project composure, became a principle I followed throughout CouBon. Whether it was restaurant churn, unpaid bills, or internal team challenges, I knew my reaction would either anchor or unravel the group. Even when the path ahead was unclear, my job was to ensure belief didn't break.

- **Momentum thrives on small wins.**
  In a startup's early stages, progress is rarely linear. There are long stretches of stagnation punctuated by brief moments of breakthrough. For us, those breakthroughs were the first restaurant onboarded, the app finally being approved, and the first user download. Each milestone, however small, served as proof that we were moving forward. I celebrated these moments relentlessly, not just for my own morale, but to remind the team that their work was bearing fruit. In environments where financial incentives are limited, emotional rewards matter even more.

Final Thoughts

Solving a two-sided marketplace isn't just a business problem; it's a belief problem. Because in the beginning, you're selling potential. You're asking one side to commit without seeing the other. You're telling restaurants that students will show up, and telling students that restaurants will too, even when neither side has any reason to believe you yet. That tension, that uncomfortable middle space, is where most marketplaces stall.

We learned early on that success wouldn't come from brute force or perfect features. It would come from a human connection. From walking door-to-door in sub-zero temperatures and showing restaurant owners that we weren't just another app trying to chip away at their margins. We were students who genuinely believed we could make our slow hours better. Success came from celebrating a 10 per cent discount deal as if it were a funding round. From learning to listen, adapt, and show up again and again, even after being ignored or rejected.

But what made this phase so formative wasn't just the sales or the signups. It was the subtle shift from idea to evidence. For the first time, people outside our circle were interacting with something we built. It was no longer hypothetical. The moment CouBon went live on the App Store, everything changed. The stakes felt real. The praise felt earned. The criticism stung deeper. And the weight of what we were trying to build became heavier, yet also more rewarding.

Still, beneath every small win was a growing sense of strain. Our energy was high, but our resources were thinning. We had momentum, but no money. We had restaurants, but still needed users. We had traction, but not yet sustainability.

This is the quiet crisis point most early-stage founders face, the space between validation and longevity. Between proving that something works and building a version of it that can last. It's where the bootstrapping hustle collides with the hard realities of bills, burn rate, and the pressure to keep moving without running out of steam.

What came next didn't just test our product. It tested our creativity, our grit, and our ability to fund a company that nobody else was quite ready to invest in. Because belief, no matter how strong, doesn't pay server costs. Passion doesn't reimburse your teammates. To keep going, we had to get resourceful in ways we never imagined, through competitions, grants, unpaid labour, and reinvesting every cent that came in.

The next phase wasn't about ambition. It was about survival. And that meant learning how to keep the lights on long enough for others to finally see what we were trying to build.

Chapter 4
No Funding, No Problem, Until It Is

As I boarded the flight back to Dubai on May 1st to begin my internship at Mubadala Capital, the investment arm of the UAE's sovereign wealth fund, my heart felt heavier than my suitcase. Before I started CouBon, my parents had made two requests: maintain strong academics (for them, that meant staying on the Dean's List) and secure top-tier internships every summer. Their reasoning was simple: if CouBon failed, I'd still have a viable safety net. I agreed, reluctantly.

Now I was about to begin my internship at one of the most prestigious firms in the region, while simultaneously preparing CouBon for its most critical phase yet. This is a tension many student founders face, balancing high-stakes academic or career commitments with the inherently volatile journey of building a startup.

Juggling Two Worlds

By 8:30 a.m., I was seated at my desk at Mubadala Capital, immersed in one of the most intellectually rigorous environments I had ever encountered. This wasn't just any internship. I was working alongside private equity veterans and ex-investment bankers from firms like Goldman Sachs, J.P. Morgan, and Moelis. Every day offered a masterclass in institutional finance, whether it was building sophisticated financial models, learning how to assess risk across global markets, or understanding how to frame a pitch in a language that resonates with professionals managing billion-dollar portfolios.

Ironically, the skills I was absorbing during the day became essential at night, when I switched hats and worked to keep CouBon alive. What I learned in the boardrooms of Mubadala helped me sound sharper in investor pitches, organise data more persuasively, and understand what a fundable business really looked like from the other side of the table.

Each morning began at 6 a.m. with Zoom calls to my team in Toronto, eight hours behind. Rick had onboarded a couple of additional developers to help streamline the app and refine the restaurant-facing backend. Meanwhile, our fledgling marketing team had started laying the groundwork for our September launch, creating social media assets, drafting pitch decks for student societies, and initiating conversations with orientation committees across Toronto universities.

After a 12-hour workday, I'd return home, make a quick dinner, and dive straight into startup mode again. Most evenings were spent identifying and reaching out to potential investors. I cold-emailed dozens of Canadian venture capitalists and angel investors. But CouBon was still too early-stage for most Canadian investors; our traction wasn't strong enough yet to spark serious interest. On the other hand, Middle Eastern investors hesitated because we were too geographically distant for them to back a student-led venture at such an early phase. The silence on both fronts was deafening.

The emotional and mental toll of balancing both lives was severe. There were days I felt like I was barely holding things together, juggling deadlines at work, trying to meet investor expectations, and keeping the team in Toronto aligned and motivated. But I developed a few systems that helped me cope, and I believe these practices can serve any student founder navigating the same balancing act:

- **Set Non-Negotiables**: At the start of each month, I mapped out key deliverables I wanted to complete. These goals were often ambitious, but ambition created momentum. I worked backwards, assigning tasks to each week, especially prioritising external-facing actions early to account for inevitable delays. Then, I broke it down into daily actions, non-negotiables that I treated with the same urgency as internship deliverables. It wasn't always comfortable, but it accelerated progress and provided clarity in chaos.
- **Maintain Regular Team Check-ins**: Weekly meetings with the CouBon team weren't just for alignment; they created external accountability. If I promised to apply to five incubators by Thursday, and we had a marketing sync on Friday, that deadline was no longer flexible. The same applied to everyone else. These meetings had a

compounding effect, with each person's punctuality encouraging the rest to raise their game.

- **Build Time Buckets, Not Overlaps**: One mental shift that helped was to treat each part of my day as its own container. When I was at Mubadala, I was fully present; I didn't let CouBon creep into my mind, no matter how tempting. And when I was in startup mode, I wasn't distracted by internship deadlines. It's tempting to multitask, but doing so fragments focus. A founder must learn to compartmentalise. As the saying goes, *"If you try to sit on two boats at once, you fall between them."*

The Turning Point

In my urgency to replenish our rapidly depleting capital, I turned to someone I hold in the highest regard, a close family friend whom I lovingly refer to as Rakesh Uncle. Once dubbed the "Casino King of Asia" during the 1990s and 2000s, Rakesh oversaw a portfolio of prominent casinos and hotel properties across the continent. Though now semi-retired, he remained actively engaged as an investor across a range of industries and geographies.

We scheduled a one-hour virtual meeting. I had spent nights crafting a polished investor deck, modelled on the ones I was reviewing at Mubadala. It covered market size, user behaviour, competitive analysis, and projected financials.

Rakesh was impressed. At the end of the call, I asked if he could connect me with anyone he thought might be genuinely interested, not just because of our relationship, but because they believed in the idea. He agreed and promised to reach out to a few long-time investment partners.

Weeks later, the call was set. On the other end of the Zoom screen were four formidable individuals, along with Rakesh himself:

- **Martin**: the Group CFO of VFS Global, the world's largest visa logistics company, and an early investor in multiple breakout startups.
- **Andries** and **Graeme**: partners in a tech-focused investment firm specialising in crypto and startup ventures. Graeme was also building a fintech app of his own.
- **Aashish**: an Indian entrepreneur with multiple F&B chains and a proven track record in early-stage angel investing.

The call lasted over three hours. I walked them through the pitch deck and fielded dozens of questions ranging from TAM projections to CAC calculations and retention strategies. They listened silently, jotting notes and cross-referencing each other's questions.

When I was asked to step out of the meeting for 15 minutes, my heart pounded. I stared at the screen, whispering mantras to stay calm.

Then came the verdict: all five of them had agreed to invest.

Investor Insights That Shaped My Pitch

In retrospect, several elements in my pitch deck likely influenced our investors' decision to commit. Many of these were drawn from my internship experience at Mubadala, where I learned firsthand how institutional investors evaluate startups, not just for feasibility, but for fundability. Here are the core principles I applied:

Understand Investor Psychology

When building my deck, I followed the Y Combinator template: Problem, Solution, How It Works, Product Screens, Go-to-Market Strategy, Key Metrics (actual or projected), Market Sizing (TAM, SAM, SOM), Competitive Landscape, and Team. But more importantly, I framed it to answer the questions that were truly on investors' minds: Is this a large enough market to justify the risk? Are these the right people to build it? Are there macro tailwinds that increase the odds of success?

Founders often pitch niche markets with modest outcomes, but early-stage investors aren't in the game for incremental wins; they're betting on outsized, asymmetric returns. Your pitch needs to credibly answer the toughest question in the room: *Can this reasonably return 10x?* If the market is too limited or the ceiling too low, even a flawless plan won't compel attention. So I was intentional in framing CouBon as a scalable opportunity with the potential for meaningful returns.

I also thought carefully about the sequencing of slides. First impressions carry weight, and in a pitch setting, placement signals confidence. Since we were first-time student founders, I knew our team slide might raise doubts, so we positioned it later in the deck. In contrast, our market sizing and strategic positioning were strong, so we led with those to establish credibility early. Structuring your deck isn't just about order; it's about narrative control.

Diligence is a Mindset, not a Checklist.

One of the starkest lessons from Mubadala was that diligence isn't just about ticking boxes; it's about identifying patterns of inconsistency. Every claim, whether about user behaviour, market sizing, or growth projections, was triangulated, challenged, and scrutinised. What I took from that was simple: *"Sloppy logic is a red flag, even if the numbers look polished."* So for CouBon, every figure in our deck had a verifiable source, every projection came with a clear rationale, and every assumption was defensible. That level of preparation projected thoughtfulness and trustworthiness, qualities far more valuable than glossy visuals or inflated forecasts.

Clarity Is a Form of Respect

At Mubadala, we routinely saw pitch decks that were 40-60 slides long. The ones that truly stood out? You could grasp the opportunity in under five minutes. That changed how I approached my own pitch. I realised: *"If your deck can't be understood quickly, you haven't done the hard thinking."* So I stripped away the fluff. I focused on why CouBon needed to exist now, the pain point we solved, and the asymmetric potential if we pulled it off. Founders often get attached to the product. But investors care more about the potential, the broader opportunity, the scalability, and the market readiness.

Storytelling Trumps Spreadsheets

Another key insight was that data alone doesn't sell, narrative does. At this stage, your numbers are largely projections. They can support your pitch, but they rarely drive it. What investors are really betting on is your vision, your understanding of the market, and your ability to tell a compelling story. CouBon wasn't just a discount platform. I framed it as: *"A marketplace that turns empty restaurant seats into revenue and gives students access to affordable meals. This isn't just about discounts, it's a shift in how local dining is optimised."* That kind of narrative sticks. It's easy to repeat, easy to remember, and invites follow-up questions.

Pre-empt Objections Before They Arise

This tactic, which I call objection anticipation, was something I picked up sitting through countless diligence calls at Mubadala. You start to recognise the questions that come up again and again, so why wait for them? For example, we had no revenue. I could've waited for someone to raise that concern, but I didn't. Instead, I led with: *"We're pre-revenue, but we've built a fully functional MVP, onboarded four restaurants during winter, and have LOIs with ten more. Execution risk is largely behind us. We're now focused on distribution."* Addressing concerns before they're raised projects control, confidence, and foresight, three things investors value enormously.

Institutional Discipline: Building Trust Through Structure

Perhaps the most underappreciated but impactful lesson I internalised was how important structure is in investor relations. At Mubadala, every portfolio company was expected to maintain a clear cadence in communication, measurable deliverables, and transparency. I replicated this discipline with CouBon's investors the moment they came on board.

What followed was two weeks of intense back-and-forth on legal contracts with our new investors. I was astounded by how diligent they were, considering the amount they invested was relatively small for them. Yet every clause, equity allocation, and repayment timeline was examined with institutional rigour. It taught me that professionalism doesn't scale with dollar amounts; it's embedded in habit.

Over time, these investors became much more than funders. They became mentors. Through these meetings and follow-up conversations, I received more dexterous and practical advice on entrepreneurship than I ever did in a classroom.

In many ways, this group became my informal board of advisors, shaping nearly every major decision CouBon made going forward. I'll always be grateful to them for taking a bet on us when all we had was conviction, a rough MVP, and a hunger to build.

But respect is a two-way street, and I knew that to keep it, I had to show up with more than gratitude. I needed to operate like the kind of founder they'd be proud to back. That started with structure. I created a simple system to track monthly KPIs, milestones, and team updates. We shared a common tracker, submitted inputs in advance, and hosted a call on the last Friday of every month to walk through progress, surface challenges, and align on next steps.

This discipline wasn't about optics; it served three core goals: it kept us accountable, brought in a valuable outside perspective, and reinforced our commitment to transparent communication.

From this rhythm emerged three golden rules for keeping early investors engaged:

1. **Be early with the bad news.** If something slipped or failed, I flagged it before the investors discovered it themselves. This not only protected trust but often brought help I hadn't expected, whether through strategic guidance or valuable connections.
2. **Create a consistent meeting cadence.** Don't just reach out when you need money or are in trouble. Regular updates build rhythm, and rhythm builds reliability. That way, investors often have your startup at the back of their mind, which can yield significant returns, such as timely introductions to potential partners, early access to grant or funding opportunities, or even strategic advice during inflection points.
3. **Share asks, not just updates.** Investors want to add value. Whether it was advice on pricing models or feedback on brand messaging, I made sure our updates always included 1-2 clear asks.

A founder's word is often their first collateral. When investors see you deliver week after week, even on small wins, it builds an unspoken currency of trust. That quiet track record of follow-through becomes one of your most powerful fundraising assets down the road.

The Character Dividend: Returning What Was Owed and Earning Institutional Backing

The very first thing I did once the investment hit our bank account in mid-July was settle the debt I owed Ethan and Daniel, the two friends who had lent me the initial $4,000 to incorporate CouBon. They were happy, but surprised. Daniel admitted that while he believed in me, he had mentally written off the loan. "Most people our age wouldn't even remember this, let alone repay it early," he said. But to me, this wasn't just about money. It was about character.

In a world where early-stage founders are often seen as risky bets, reputation becomes your first real currency. When someone places faith in you, whether with their money, time, or trust, honouring that commitment speaks louder than any pitch deck. I've come to believe that capital follows character. Over the course of CouBon's journey, this quiet credibility became one of my greatest assets. When I needed support again, whether it was from teammates, mentors, or future investors, those early actions echoed.

That growing reputation also opened doors to institutional support. As CouBon gained momentum, I began applying to university-affiliated incubators and accelerators around Toronto, not just for funding, but for the structure and validation they could offer. These programs didn't just hand out cheques; they amplified our credibility. We were accepted into several, with some being:

1. **University of Toronto's Centre for Entrepreneurship**, one of the largest incubators in Canada, which not only gave us mentorship but also a co-working space
2. **Bridge Incubator at the University of Toronto**, where we received a regular stipend of $1,000 for marketing
3. **Toronto Metropolitan University's Science and Discovery Zone**, which helped us reach a wider student base outside of the University of Toronto

These affiliations weren't just symbolic. They gave CouBon institutional grounding. Suddenly, we weren't just a few students building something in our dorm rooms; we were part of a larger ecosystem, recognised by credible entities. That external validation mattered, not just for PR, but because it signalled to future stakeholders that CouBon had momentum and was worth taking seriously.

By the end of July, I had wrapped up my internship, secured our first round of funding, repaid those who had believed in me when we had nothing, and aligned CouBon with institutions that gave us credibility. The months ahead, leading into our official September launch, would be some of the most defining. But with character as our foundation and structure as our scaffolding, we were finally ready to scale.

Final Thoughts

Funding is often romanticised as a finish line, proof that your idea matters, your story sells, and your execution can scale. But that illusion fades quickly. Capital doesn't validate your business. It just exposes it.

What those early months taught me, across pitch calls, investor meetings, and late-night strategy sessions, is that getting someone to believe in you is just the first test. The harder one is proving they were right to. A wire transfer is a starting gun, not a trophy.

CouBon was no longer just an experiment. We had investors, incubators, and a mission that had outgrown the Google Docs and dorm room debates it began with. We had also built something rarer than a strong pitch; we had earned trust. That quiet capital, built on consistency and follow-through, would serve us long after the money ran dry.

By the end of July, I had wrapped up my internship, secured our first round of funding, repaid those who had believed in me when we had nothing, and aligned CouBon with institutions that gave us credibility. It felt like the culmination of a chapter, but in truth, it was just the clearing of the runway. The months ahead, leading into our official September launch, would be some of the most defining. But with character as our foundation and structure as our scaffolding, we were finally ready to scale.

Still, for all the spreadsheets and strategy, one truth remained: CouBon wasn't yet working the way it needed to. The metrics looked good on a pitch deck, but user behaviour told a more sobering story. Downloads were climbing, but retention was shallow. The app was being opened, but not often revisited. We had movement, but not momentum.

And that was the real work ahead, not just building, but making it *stick*.

The question was no longer *Can we raise money?* It was, *Can we justify it?*

That meant confronting uncomfortable truths about product-market fit, student behaviour, and what it really takes to convert early hype into lasting traction. That's what came next. And that's what turned CouBon from a project into a real company.

Chapter 5
Your Startup's Not a Startup, it's a Project Until It's Working

The task ahead of us was monumental. With newly raised capital, we now had the fuel to launch. All we needed to do was take off.

I landed back in Toronto in August, a few weeks before classes began. We had our eyes on orientation week, a sea of first-year students entering universities across the city. Each campus organised multiple events to welcome them, and students were in that rare state of openness: eager to explore, discover, and try new things.

The timing was perfect. But the challenge? We weren't big enough for any university to take us seriously. Looking back, that was a blessing in disguise. Because what we lacked in official support, we made up for with sheer scrappiness. The cards we were dealt weren't great, but that didn't mean we couldn't win the hand; we just had to bluff well enough to stay in the game.

I discovered that the University of Toronto was hosting its annual Club Fair in two days. This was a massive event; St. George Street would be closed, and hundreds of clubs would be setting up booths to attract new students. I reached out to the organisers but was turned away. "Clubs only," they said. No space for startups.

So we hacked it.

The booths all used plain white tables. The night before, I went to IKEA and bought one that looked the same. We had already printed a CouBon banner, so the next morning, we set up shop at the very end of the street. It looked legit enough, and if anyone asked, we'd say we were part of an incubator, hoping they didn't ask which one.

The move worked. That one table, placed without permission, became the ignition point for CouBon's presence across Toronto campuses.

Looking back, that IKEA table wasn't just a hack; it was a metaphor. As a student founder, you rarely get permission. You create legitimacy through audacity. That moment taught me something I carry with me today: credibility isn't granted; it's taken. Whether it's bootstrapping without approval or reaching out to mentors above your weight class, progress in the early days is less about access and more about initiative.

Over the next 10 days, we did the same at Toronto Metropolitan and York University. We weren't granted permission, but we acted like we belonged, setting up booths, printing flyers, and pitching students. By the end of orientation, we had attended over seven events and spent more than 50 hours in the sun. My arms had a tan like I'd been vacationing on a beach, not grinding in concrete courtyards.

But it worked.

We spoke to over 1,000 students. We crossed 500 downloads. CouBon even trended in the top 100 apps on the Canadian App Store and Play Store.

Beyond the Booth: Experimenting with Growth Hacks

The momentum was thrilling. And we didn't stop. We kicked off with an all-out campus marketing campaign. Flyers were plastered across dormitory lobbies, cafeteria walls, lecture halls, and library entrances, on any flat surface we could get our hands on. We printed in bulk, worked late nights taping them up, and checked back the next day, only to find most had already been torn down or removed by university staff. Printing costs added up quickly, and engagement was nearly impossible to track. In retrospect, it was more motion than impact. A well-intentioned hustle, but hardly a scalable strategy.

Then came the absurd. In a bid to cut through the noise, I started announcing CouBon on Toronto's subway system and filming it. The goal wasn't to target commuters; our users were students. The idea was to create virality through contrast. If someone saw a suited-up guy passionately pitching a student discount app in a packed metro, maybe they'd pause, laugh, and share. Maybe it would catch fire. And it did, briefly. The videos racked up likes, shares, and DMs. My friends were baffled. Even my team thought I had finally tipped over the edge onto the craziness spectrum.

But the attention was misleading. The views came, the clout followed, but the downloads didn't. Our app store metrics barely moved. That disconnect was sobering. It reminded me that going viral isn't the same as going valuable. And in early-stage startups, there's a fine line between clever marketing and performative energy burn.

We also tried something more grassroots, pitching CouBon directly in classrooms. I had built good relationships with several professors across departments, and they kindly gave us a minute or two before their lectures to speak to the class. It seemed like a golden opportunity; students gathered in one place, with attention pointed forward. But the reality was different. Most students were mentally checked out before the first slide even loaded. We became background noise. Still, because the cost was negligible, just a bit of time and social capital, we kept doing it. Even a handful of conversions justified the effort.

Amid all these flashy and not-so-flashy attempts, one truth began to emerge consistency quietly outperformed creativity.

We started leaning into the "Rule of 7" in marketing, the idea that a consumer needs seven encounters with a brand before they engage. We weren't banking on a single big moment. Instead, we focused on being everywhere: CouBon flyers on every noticeboard that didn't get cleaned daily, Instagram reels optimised for student humour, casual mentions during club fair conversations, and recurring posts in campus messaging groups. Not every touchpoint converted, but each added a subtle layer of familiarity. By the end of September, the name CouBon didn't need explanation; it sparked recognition.

When we finally crossed 1,000 downloads, it felt like more than just a number. It was proof that momentum could be engineered, not through gimmicks alone, but through thoughtful, repeated visibility. It wasn't sexy. It wasn't viral. But it worked.

That moment offered us something precious: an early product-market fit *signal*. Not confirmation, not certainty, but a flicker that we were solving a real need, in a way students were willing to try.

The October Reality Check: Growth Without Retention Isn't Growth

We were so focused on acquisition, we didn't notice the hole in our bucket.

Our daily active users didn't match our download numbers. Users downloaded the app, but they weren't redeeming discounts. And restaurants, having been promised increased foot traffic, were starting to lose patience.

I decided to walk through the user journey:

1. Download the app
2. Open it and browse the discounts
3. Go to a restaurant
4. Order a meal
5. Get a 6-digit code from the server
6. Enter that code in the app to activate the discount

In this user experience, we had a few concrete data points, namely: when they downloaded the app, when they opened it and browsed specific discounts, and when they entered the 6-digit code to 'redeem' the discount. The backend showed a steep drop-off between step 3 and step 6. So we mystery shopped ourselves. I visited the restaurants posing as a regular customer.

And I found the issue.

Many of the restaurant staff had no idea what CouBon was. In some cases, the owner had briefly told the manager, who didn't relay the message to the waitstaff. In others, the staff just forgot. Some were apathetic and simply did not care enough.

We called the owners and asked them to better train their teams.

Still, nothing changed.

So we started visiting each restaurant ourselves, biweekly at first, training their staff. We printed out flyers and taped them behind cash registers. Still, nothing. One worker looked at me blankly as I showed her the flyer; she didn't even glance at the instructions taped next to her.

After two months of effort, the issue persisted. That's when it hit me. The problem wasn't worker incompetence; it was structural. We had built a system dependent on third-party execution, and those third parties weren't aligned.

Most of our restaurant partners were small, independently owned, and often lacked formal operations. Staff turnover was high. Training was ad hoc. And we were expecting precision from a chaotic system.

In hindsight, several hard-earned lessons emerged, insights that, had I understood earlier, might have spared us many of the teething issues we encountered. Here are some of the most critical takeaways.

Lessons from the Drop-Off

1. **Run a Real Pilot, not a Launch in Disguise.**
   Before scaling anything, test it under real-world conditions. We should've started with 2-3 carefully selected restaurants and a few dozen students *outside* our friend circle. A true pilot isn't just about usage; it's about stress-testing every assumption in a live environment: Will users understand the value? Will staff actually cooperate? Where do drop-offs happen, and why? We skipped this in our rush to "go live," and paid the price later. Pilots buy you time to iterate quietly, before the spotlight (and expectations) arrive.

2. **Control the User Experience, End-to-End**
   Our biggest mistake was depending on external actors, namely restaurant staff, to deliver a consistent experience. That variability proved fatal. The lesson? Minimise external dependencies wherever possible. Whether it's a code redemption process or customer onboarding, the more you control, the more predictability you gain. This principle extends beyond CouBon. Look at Uber, they moved towards in-app tipping and auto-routing, not just for convenience, but to reduce human inconsistency. Ownership of key touchpoints is what separates reliable platforms from chaotic ones.

3. **Escape the Friend Feedback Trap**
   It's natural to test with friends first. But this creates a warped sense of readiness. Friends tend to be supportive, overly patient, and forgiving of flaws. Real users won't be. If they're confused, they'll leave and never tell you why. To get honest feedback, you have to test in the wild. Create feedback loops that force objectivity: run blind usability tests, or observe

someone using your app without explanation. You'll learn more in one hour of real-world friction than in a hundred supportive conversations.

4. **Simplify, Ruthlessly**

   If your product requires more than 10 seconds to explain to a stranger, it's too complex. Period. We built a multi-step redemption process that seemed logical to us, but introduced friction at every turn. Each additional tap, form, or verbal instruction is an invitation for drop-off. Simplicity isn't just good UX, it's essential for survival, especially in early-stage products. A streamlined flow converts better, trains faster, and breaks less often.

When the Downloads Dropped to 200

Despite our initial spike, by December our active user base had shrunk to just 200.

Restaurants were threatening to leave. Investors were growing restless. Team morale was quickly unravelling. I could feel the foundation cracking beneath me.

Rick, our CTO, was immersed in code, scrambling to fix technical bugs. Ali, our head of partnerships, was doing everything in his power to retain restaurant relationships. Our marketing team, driven but made up of full-time students, was running on fumes as final exams loomed. And I was caught in the centre of it all, juggling investor check-ins, internal doubts, mounting academic deadlines, and the creeping weight of burnout.

Final exams were approaching fast. Assignments were piling up. My GPA, something I had promised my parents I'd never compromise, suddenly felt like a distant afterthought. This is the part most people miss about student founders: you're not just building a startup. You're also trying to stay afloat in school. While running a company under pressure, I was also expected to submit essays, revise for midterms, and show up to class as if nothing was falling apart.

There were nights I'd sit alone in my room, staring blankly at spreadsheets, drowning in doubt. I didn't want to share this with Rick; he was already overwhelmed. My friends were supportive, but I knew they couldn't fully understand. It wasn't a lack of empathy, just a lack of lived experience. And my parents, though deeply caring, came from the corporate world. Their logic was clean-cut: *"If it's draining you this much, maybe it's time to take a break. Focus on school."*

But CouBon wasn't a school club or a summer hobby. It had become part of who I was, something I had poured belief, sacrifice, and sleepless nights into. It wasn't just a business. It was a responsibility I wasn't ready to walk away from.

So, I pushed through, not out of blind optimism, but out of necessity. This wasn't about dreaming big anymore. It was about surviving long enough to build something worth dreaming about.

Every hour I spent fixing CouBon was an hour I wasn't preparing for internships, keeping up with readings, or simply sleeping. There's a hidden tax to being a student founder that no one warns you about: opportunity cost. While my peers were polishing resumes, attending finance networking mixers, or practising case interviews, I was pounding pavements, securing new restaurant partnerships, fixing leaky parts of our model, and holding together a wobbling startup.

There were moments I questioned if the trade-off was worth it. Was missing a shot at a top-tier internship or falling slightly behind in my academic track record the right call? But deep down, I knew I'd make the same decision again. The experiences CouBon gave me, the pressure of leadership, the grit of problem-solving, and the firsthand exposure to markets, people, and failures were teaching me more than any summer analyst stint ever could. Maybe it wouldn't reflect immediately in my GPA or LinkedIn, but in the long run, these were the exact skills that would set me apart, not just as a student, but as a future builder.

During those difficult months, I leaned on a few tools and mental frameworks that helped me stay grounded and push through the chaos, tools I now believe every student founder should keep in their arsenal.

Tools I Used to Stay Afloat

Mental compartmentalisation - I learned to create mental boundaries. I couldn't afford to be emotionally hijacked all day, so I gave myself permission to worry, but only during certain windows. After midnight, no spiralling. This rule wasn't just about peace of mind; it was about energy conservation. Anxiety drains clarity, and I needed every ounce of clarity to make decisions under pressure.

Micro-goals - In a world where everything felt broken, progress had to be manufactured. I set three non-negotiable goals each week: small, concrete wins that I could control. These goals acted like emotional lifebuoys. They gave me proof that I was moving forward, even when the bigger picture felt stagnant or uncertain.

Team check-ins - When chaos reigns, people crave rhythm. I established weekly team calls, not just to assign tasks, but to create psychological safety. These meetings reconnected us to our mission, clarified our next moves, and reminded everyone that we weren't in this alone. Even when morale dipped, the act of showing up for one another became its own form of accountability.

Silence sprints - When the noise got too loud, I unplugged, completely. No Slack, no emails, no group chats. Just a few hours of intentional silence where I could think clearly, without input or interruption. These sprints became my most productive windows. The irony was clear: to lead publicly, I first had to retreat privately.

Learning from others - I turned to founder memoirs, startup podcasts, and long-form interviews. Hearing how other entrepreneurs navigated existential lows gave me both perspective and permission to feel lost, to screw up, and to keep going anyway. I realised that the chaos I was in wasn't proof that I was failing. It was proof I was trying. Their stories made mine feel less like a crisis and more like a chapter. A brutal one, yes, but one I wasn't alone in writing.

Final Thoughts

By December, the energy that once fuelled CouBon had begun to dim. What started with late nights, early wins, and a team high on belief was now strained by unmet expectations, stagnant metrics, and silent users. Our download numbers had flatlined. Restaurants that once welcomed us with cautious optimism began voicing concerns, or worse, disengaging altogether. The internal Slack channels were quieter, morale was brittle, and the mounting pressure had shifted from possibility to preservation.

I often found myself staring at dashboards late into the night, refreshing numbers that refused to change, replaying conversations with partners who sounded less certain than they once did. It wasn't just professional disappointment; it was personal disorientation. When you pour so much of your identity into something, watching it falter feels like a private unravelling.

But buried within that difficult December was something else. Not hope, not breakthrough, something quieter and more useful: clarity.

The problem wasn't surface-level. It wasn't about needing more ad spend or social media engagement or clever promotions. Our marketing hadn't failed us;

our model had. We had succeeded in making noise, but not in designing a system that converted that attention into action. We had built an experience that was, at its core, disconnected from how students actually behaved, from how restaurants preferred to operate, and from how trust is formed in a transactional ecosystem.

What felt like a collapse was, in hindsight, a critical diagnosis. A sobering mirror. One who asked uncomfortable but necessary questions:

- Why were users dropping off after a single redemption?
- Why did restaurants feel underwhelmed, even when the numbers looked promising on paper?
- Why did every operational hiccup feel like a structural failure rather than a solvable glitch?

The answers weren't flattering. We had delegated too much of the fulfilment to external players, restaurant staff who had little incentive to ensure a good user experience. We had overestimated the power of discounts and underestimated the friction of human behaviour. We had built systems on trust and good intentions instead of operational discipline and feedback loops.

And perhaps most crucially, we had treated downloads as traction, instead of measuring true engagement and retention.

This period was my first real lesson in startup maturity: the shift from building with emotion to building with precision. It's easy to conflate motion with progress when early wins mask deeper flaws. It's harder, but far more necessary, to pause and ask whether your assumptions are still valid, or whether your entire approach needs to evolve.

What we were running wasn't yet a business. It was a project. A compelling one, yes, but a project nonetheless. Projects live on hope and effort. Companies live on systems and outcomes. That was the inflection point we had reached: not whether to continue, but whether we had the courage to unlearn and rebuild.

I look back on that winter not with regret, but with a quiet respect. Because that was the moment CouBon stopped being a side hustle and started becoming something real, not because we were growing, but because we were willing to change.

Not every chapter in entrepreneurship ends with a win. But some end with a mirror. And if you're honest enough to look into it, that reflection can become your most powerful lever.

We hadn't lost the will to build. What we had gained, through trial, error, and near-burnout, was the wisdom to build better.

CouBon
The Camera Roll Edition

CouBon Logo

Boothing in one of CouBon's first orientation events on September 23. In the picture are some of the early team members, starting from left: Alex, Rick, Julian, Tejas, and Matteo

Tejas promoting CouBon in a large lecture course

Tejas promoting CouBon at a student association event.

Tejas promoting CouBon at an entrepreneurship event

Invited to the annual entrepreneurship show. From left: Rick, Yashi, Tejas

Tejas having a strategic meeting with some of CouBon's angel investors. From left to right: Graeme, Martin, Tejas

Ali promoting CouBon at an orientation event

Large crowd around our booth, showing their love.

Students promoting CouBon!

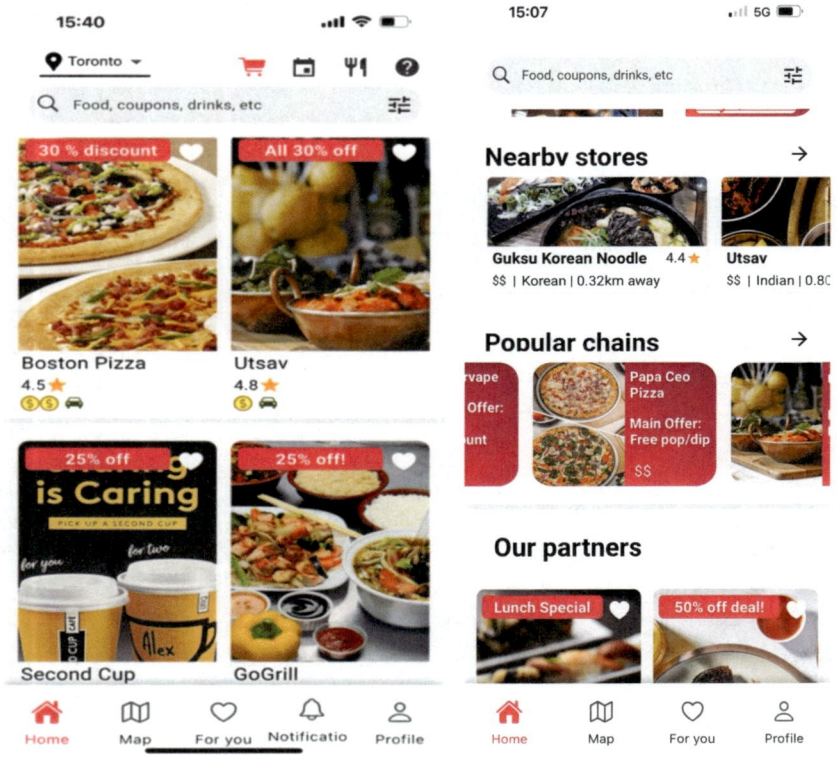

UX interface of our app, showing partnered brands like Second Cup & Boston Pizza

Behind the scenes, an extended CouBon team photo

*Behind the scenes after a long day of marketing events.
From left to right: Yashi, Rick, Ali, Tejas*

Keita promoting CouBon at a tech conference

CouBon makes it to the top 100 apps on the Canadian App Store

On the left is a flyer for CouBon. On the right is an advert on Blog Toronto, one of the most widely read magazines in the city.

CouBon being taught as a marketing case study in class.

Tejas promoting CouBon in the City Metro.

Partnered restaurants getting sales in our organised Science Rendezvous event

Chapter 6
Growth Isn't Traction, Until It's Sustainable

We launched CouBon's new model in February 2024, and everything about it was different.

Gone were the old days of hoping restaurant staff would remember a code. Now, we have shifted to a fully trackable system. Users would pre-pay through the app, money would flow to us via Stripe, a payment gateway widely used by startups, and every Friday, we'd transfer the collected revenue to each restaurant. The lag in payment wasn't ideal, but given the low transaction volumes initially, most restaurants accepted it. For those who didn't, I personally met them and explained why this change was necessary.

We needed control.

This new model allowed us to track every metric, from visits to redemptions, without relying on restaurant staff. More importantly, it gave us room to subsidise discounts directly and selectively during promotional periods. A 50% discount, even if unsustainable long-term, was a hook. It lowered the bar for first-time users and allowed us to build trust.

Rebuilding with Less, But Smarter

Our relaunch included fewer restaurants, but the experience was drastically improved. The interface was smoother, discounts were bigger, and the process was simpler. We launched with bated breath.

In late February, the first trickle of transactions came in: 50 payments, 150 new downloads. March saw stronger growth, and by April, we hit 500 transactions per month. It felt like the product finally had legs.

But it wasn't time to celebrate just yet.

The First Taste of Unit Economics

This was the phase where CouBon began to mature, from a passionate project into an operationally grounded startup. And that transition started with confronting the harsh realities of our numbers.

The initial relaunch had brought encouraging momentum. Downloads were up, usage was growing, and the CouBon brand was becoming recognisable across campus. But there was a looming problem: we were bleeding cash. For every discounted transaction, we were subsidising a sizable portion, sometimes up to 40%. A $20 meal would feature a $10 discount, of which only $2 came from the restaurant. The remaining $8 came from our own limited reserves. While this model catalysed user growth, it was fundamentally unsustainable.

So we had to evolve, fast.

With new traction serving as social proof, I started targeting better-known restaurant chains; brands that students already recognised and trusted. This wasn't just about optics. Chains like Boston Pizza, Second Cup Coffee, Tahini's, and Burger Factory brought structure and professionalism. Their staff were already trained in handling third-party platforms, which reduced operational friction. More importantly, partnering with such names gave us the legitimacy we needed to convince others to join.

But onboarding larger partners required a shift in narrative. It was no longer enough to talk about CouBon as a scrappy student project. I began approaching owners and managers with data: user demographics, growth curves, transaction frequency, and student feedback. I framed CouBon not as a discount gimmick, but as a tool to drive foot traffic during off-peak hours – a value-add that complemented their existing business cycles. For many, that clicked.

And it allowed us to do something we hadn't done before: charge.

Up to this point, restaurants weren't paying us a dime. We were facilitating transactions and subsidising discounts without earning revenue. Now, with stronger traction and established names on the platform, I reintroduced our business model: a 10% commission on post-discount revenue.

It wasn't an easy sell. Some owners pushed back. So I piloted a tiered approach. For newer partners, the first 1-2 weeks were free. Once they saw results, measurable increases in off-peak orders and higher student footfall, they were more willing to pay the commission. At the same time, we needed to reduce our burn, and that meant decreasing the size of our subsidies.

Initially, CouBon offered deep discounts (often 40-50%) to drive urgency and adoption. But now, with restaurants contributing more and the app gaining traction, I decided to experiment with smaller discount amounts. On certain days or at specific locations, we quietly dropped the offered discount from 40% to 25% or even 20%, then monitored transaction volumes.

Would users still redeem?

Surprisingly, many did. While redemption rates dipped slightly, the drop wasn't nearly as steep as we had feared. It revealed something important: for a growing segment of our user base, CouBon had become a habit. Students weren't just chasing the biggest discount anymore; they were using CouBon because it had become part of their dining routine. This was a sticky demand. And it gave us breathing room.

By May, we had recalibrated our unit economics. The average discount dropped to around 25%, of which we were only subsidising 5% on the app, and in return, earned a commission of 10%.

The result?

We became operationally cash-flow positive. That didn't mean we were profitable, far from it. But our burn was now deliberate, not desperate. Each dollar spent had a purpose, and each campaign had a feedback loop.

More than just a financial shift, this period taught me something deeper: that sustainable growth isn't just about momentum, it's about margin. And unless a startup figures out how to make money while it grows, that growth is just a countdown clock disguised as progress.

Bridge Round vs. Ownership Sprawl

By mid-April, as traction increased and our unit economics started trending positive, it became clear that CouBon was on firmer footing. But the very momentum we had worked so hard to create brought a new challenge: we were burning cash faster than we could stabilise. The 10% commission model and reduced discounts helped, but they hadn't fully kicked in yet. We were still subsidising user growth, onboarding new restaurants, and ramping up our student outreach. It was working, but it was expensive.

By April, we had crossed 1,500 downloads and were seeing a steady uptick in recurring users. The app wasn't just being downloaded; it was being used. Redemptions were happening daily, restaurants were reporting new student customers, and CouBon had started to resemble a machine, not a leaky bucket.

But that momentum brought with it an unexpected problem: we were growing faster than we had planned, and burning faster too.

The subsidies that had helped drive early traction were now multiplying. Every new user was a win for engagement but a loss for the balance sheet. The very success we had worked so hard to manufacture was now threatening to outpace our ability to sustain it. At our current burn rate, we have maybe two months of runway left. And with the summer season around the corner, a natural lull for campus-centric businesses, I couldn't afford to wait.

We needed more capital, and we needed it urgently.

That's when I made the decision to raise a bridge round, a small infusion of capital from our existing investors to help us extend our runway and carry momentum into the next growth cycle. But I was intentional about how we framed it. This wasn't a panic raise. It was a measured ask at a slightly higher valuation, justified by the traction we had built and the milestones we had hit.

The conversations were surprisingly swift. Because our investor communications had been regular and transparent, our backers weren't caught off guard. They had been following our progress, monthly KPIs, user growth, and restaurant expansions, and had seen the groundwork laid for this next step. They understood what this capital would unlock, and more importantly, they believed in our discipline as stewards of their money.

Within 48 hours, the funds were wired. No overcomplicated due diligence. No drawn-out negotiations. Just trust. That experience reaffirmed a lesson I've come to hold closely: fast money follows quiet credibility.

We did have other funding options. A few restaurant partners had expressed interest in investing. On paper, it sounded ideal, turning vendors into stakeholders. But I resisted. As flattering as it was, I knew that spreading equity too thin, too early, could hurt us later.

Institutional investors expect clean cap tables. And operationally, having too many voices at the table, even well-meaning ones, slows decision-making and increases friction. In startups, agility is a currency, and I didn't want to dilute that. Equity is your sharpest tool as a founder; giving it away without strategy is like trading future control for present comfort. I chose to preserve that leverage for future rounds, when CouBon would be in a stronger position and the capital raised could be even more catalytic.

This bridge round wasn't just about buying time; it was about buying options. It allowed us to finish the semester strong, experiment more boldly with our monetisation strategies, and build the kind of track record that would attract more institutional capital later. We weren't just surviving; we were starting to scale with intent.

But traction doesn't quell criticism; it amplifies it. The more visible we became, the more scrutiny we attracted. Suddenly, CouBon wasn't just a scrappy startup run by students; it was a growing platform, and with that came opinions. Everyone had advice. Everyone had feedback. And most of it sounded the same.

The Feedback No One Warns You About

During this time, we received a recurring piece of vague feedback: *"Get better restaurants. Do more marketing."* That stung, not because it was wrong, but because it dismissed the execution behind the scenes. What those comments overlooked was the invisible grind that had brought us this far.

No one saw me standing outside in the middle of a snowstorm, pitching to franchise owners who barely made eye contact. No one sat through the six-coffee negotiations or watched me navigate contract clauses with restaurant managers who had never heard of CouBon, let alone trusted it. They didn't see the days spent troubleshooting tech issues at storefronts, or the effort it took to keep newly onboarded staff from ignoring the platform when it mattered most. They saw the result, and if it wasn't impressive, the assumption was that we simply weren't trying hard enough.

But that's the brutal honesty of building something real: effort is invisible. Customers don't reward you for how hard you work. Investors don't care how many calls it took to close a deal. You're not judged by the mountain you climbed, you're judged by whether or not you got there.

Once I accepted that truth, my relationship with feedback changed. I stopped taking it personally and started listening to what it was trying to tell me. Feedback isn't always well-phrased, but it's almost always directionally useful, if you can decode it. "Get better restaurants" didn't mean we were lazy. It meant our brand partners didn't inspire enough confidence. "Do more marketing" wasn't an insult. It was a symptom; people hadn't seen us enough, or remembered us when they did.

Ironically, just as we were navigating this internal complexity, CouBon was becoming a visible name on campus. Our branding popped up in conversations, group chats, and even casual classroom banter.

Students began to refer to us as *"that startup with the food discounts."* We had a booth at nearly every campus event. People took notice.

What we didn't expect, however, was that CouBon would end up being studied in Master's level business courses, while I, its founder, was still an undergrad. In one class, a professor dissected our model as a live case of a two-sided marketplace in its early stages. Another used our traction challenges to discuss the risks of customer-side subsidies.

But nothing topped the moment we saw CouBon featured as a case study in our own Operations Management exam. Neither Ali nor I had any idea this would happen. We stared at the question in disbelief, then did the unthinkable: we got it wrong! We, the people who built the company from scratch, misunderstood the logic the professor had applied to our own business. It was both hilarious and humbling.

That moment has stuck with me ever since, not because it exposed a flaw in our understanding, but because it reflected a deeper truth of startup life: even when the story is yours, even when you *lived* the data and shaped the decisions, success isn't about knowing, it's about executing. It's about clarity in context. And sometimes, even the founder needs a second look to see the full picture.

Professionalism Isn't Universal

As CouBon began scaling, one of the unexpected challenges wasn't growth; it was the *drag* caused by partners we had onboarded too early.

Some of our first restaurant partners had been generous, enthusiastic, and willing to take a bet on us when we had nothing but an idea and a Google Form. For that, I was (and still am) deeply grateful. But as we moved into a more structured, data-driven phase, it became increasingly clear that not all partnerships were created equal. Professionalism, I learned, wasn't universal.

We started noticing a troubling trend: a cluster of refund requests tied to one particular franchise partner. Students would go to redeem their CouBon offer, and staff on-site would either deny the discount outright or act confused, pretending they'd never heard of the platform. What should have been a seamless win-win became a chaotic, embarrassing experience for users and a logistical mess for us.

Each complaint took time to resolve. Our tiny customer support function (i.e., me and one team member) would have to cross-verify transactions, call the restaurant, explain the situation, and then issue a refund, often eating the cost ourselves just to protect the user experience. It was death by a thousand cuts. Refund by refund, we were bleeding both money and trust.

At first, I chalked it up to poor training. Maybe the staff hadn't been properly briefed. So I reached out to the owner. I was polite, assuming this could be resolved with a few reminders and a short retraining call.

Instead, I was met with hostility.

The owner was defensive from the start. He accused us of confusing his staff, of making false promises, even of *"sending too many students"* who *"only wanted free food."* I was stunned. We were literally delivering him paying customers, and yet, somehow, *we* were the problem.

I'll be honest, I was seething. Not just because of the rudeness, but because of the disrespect to our users and the disinterest in fixing it. I had every reason to go on the offensive. I had screenshots, complaints, and timestamps. But I didn't.

Because here's the uncomfortable truth I learned: in business, professionalism isn't always reciprocated. But your response still defines you.

There's a rule I started living by that day: don't burn bridges, unless you're absolutely sure you'll never need to cross that river again.

So we took a different approach. I offboarded them quietly. We removed them from the app, issued a polite statement to our users citing "partner process inconsistencies," and moved on. No public call-outs. No bad-mouthing. Just clarity, closure, and a cleaner experience for our customers.

Why? Because the short-term satisfaction of "winning" the argument wasn't worth the long-term consequences. The F&B industry is surprisingly interconnected. Word travels fast, especially bad words. And even if I never worked with that owner again, I didn't want him to poison our name in his network. Reputation, once lost, is painfully hard to rebuild.

What that episode taught me was simple but critical: startups don't just need partners, they need professional partners. Reliability matters. Operational follow-through matters. And when you're growing fast, every weak link multiplies friction.

As CouBon matured, we began implementing minimum partner standards. Clear onboarding processes, staff training kits, signage for visibility, and mid-month check-ins became the norm. We shifted from *"please give us a chance"* to *"this is how we operate"*, not out of arrogance, but out of necessity. The platform wasn't a scrappy project anymore. It was becoming a system. And systems break when one part doesn't hold up.

Operational Depth: Building a Real Team

Once CouBon's product began to stabilise and our early traction turned from fluke to repeatable pattern, I realised that brute force and founder hustle alone wouldn't carry us much further. The system we were building needed scaffolding, not just in code or process, but in *people*. So I shifted my focus inward: it was time to build a real team.

But I approached this phase with one important lesson in mind: *startups don't have the luxury of hiring for potential alone*. Every person brought in had to make the machine run faster, cleaner, or smarter *from day one*. This wasn't about filling roles for optics; it was about operational necessity.

One of the first hires during this phase was Meer, whom I had worked with on previous campus initiatives. He wasn't just sharp, he was methodical, precise, and intensely self-driven. I put him in charge of building out CouBon's first data analytics function. Until that point, we were making too many product and marketing decisions based on anecdote or instinct. But Meer changed that.

He began by centralising our fragmented data sources: scraping together Stripe logs, in-app event histories, marketing funnel data, and even user feedback forms. Then, using simple dashboards, he helped us move from reactive decisions to data-informed experimentation. We started tracking when redemptions peaked (usually Thursdays), which discount percentages triggered impulse redemptions, and how retention shifted based on time-of-day pushes.

One key insight from his work: students were far more responsive to limited-time offers that expired within hours than they were to static daily discounts. That single realisation changed how we structured the app interface and our notification system.

Parallel to the data buildout, we began professionalising our marketing efforts, which, until then, were mostly ad hoc: last-minute flyers, Instagram posts made on Canva at midnight, and stunts like metro announcements filmed on my phone.

Enter Yashi, someone who had followed CouBon's journey closely and genuinely believed in the mission. What stood out about her wasn't just her creative skillset, but her operational consistency. She created campaign calendars, structured feedback loops between marketing and data, and started framing content around measurable outcomes, not just aesthetics.

What emerged over those weeks wasn't just a bigger team; it was a *real organisation*. We grew to a lean unit of ten people, each with a defined role, a dashboard of responsibilities, and ownership over outcomes. We weren't just doing tasks anymore; we were solving problems with the process. Regular syncs replaced random check-ins. Asana boards replaced scattered to-do lists. And slowly, the language of the team changed from *"Can someone take care of this?"* to *"Let's review what worked and why."*

I saw the difference in morale, too. When people know their scope, feel their impact, and trust the people around them, work stops feeling like a scramble and starts feeling like momentum.

CouBon was no longer a project duct-taped together by a couple of founders running on adrenaline. We were becoming a functioning operation – with systems, insights, and people who didn't just believe in the vision, but were helping to architect it.

What I Learned: Growth Is a System, Not a Spike

The months following our relaunch weren't just about fixing what was broken. They were about laying the groundwork for a system that could eventually scale without imploding.

Here are some takeaways I now live by:

- **Control your metrics before you chase them.** At first, I was obsessed with flashy KPIs, downloads, social media reach, and campus buzz. But I realised none of that mattered if users weren't transacting. I remember one week we hit 300 new downloads, and I thought we'd turned a corner. Then I checked: only four redemptions. It was humbling. From then on, I made it a ritual to track usage funnels first, then figure out where people were dropping off. For any student startup, the sooner you link growth with behaviour, not vanity, the better.
- **Ensure you are building growth, not buying it:** For first-time founders, it's easy to get excited when traction picks up and start burning cash to accelerate it, without a clear exit plan. But growth fuelled purely by subsidies or promotions is unsustainable unless it's part of a deliberate strategy. You need to know exactly what the spend is

achieving and how you'll phase it out while retaining the gains. In CouBon's case, I was intentional about subsidising discounts for a few months. The goal wasn't just to attract users; it was to create enough momentum to bring better restaurant partners on board, negotiate stronger deals, and use that improved offering to drive organic retention. That strategy ultimately allowed us to transition into a cash-flow positive model.

- **Professionalise early.** Clear team structures ensure internal accountability. As students with limited work experience, your team will often struggle with the sense of discipline that larger firms may have. As such, having clearly demarcated teams with team leads puts the onus on the team lead to ensure their team works effectively, creating efficient delegation. Furthermore, use data to inform the majority of your strategic decisions, for it often tells a story we as founders may overlook in the chaos. For CouBon, it was important to measure the success of our discount subsidy initiative, as well as gauge when demand would be sticky enough for us to reduce the subsidy we offered. Data played a key role in giving us this insight by showing increases in usage as well as the repetition of discount redemptions when we reduced the discounts temporarily.

- **Equity is leverage. Use it wisely.** Don't give it away too freely. Ownership affects control and culture. Many first-time (especially student) founders undervalue the importance of cap table cleanliness. I almost made the mistake of accepting investment from multiple restaurants just because they offered quick capital. But giving 1-2% here and there without long-term alignment is dangerous; it not only complicates governance but also scares away institutional investors later. A mentor once told me, *"Every per cent you give away is a vote you sell."* That stuck with me. I learned to treat equity as more than money, its influence, agility, and future leverage. Especially as a young founder, retaining control isn't just about power; it's about clarity of direction.

And most importantly:

- **How to Know If The Idea Is Working:** The truth is, most early-stage student startups don't need explosive user growth; they need signs of momentum. I learned this the hard way. During CouBon's early relaunch, I kept wondering: is this still just a passion project, or are we building a real business? The first clear sign came when users started coming back without reminders. Students began using CouBon multiple times a week, not just once out of curiosity. They weren't deleting the app; they were forming a habit. The second sign was when restaurants began reaching out to us. Initially, we were pitching door to door, trying to convince sceptical owners. But slowly, through student referrals or competing franchise chatter, restaurant owners began emailing us first. That shift from chasing to being chased was massive. And finally, the biggest sign wasn't external at all. It was within the team. When people started spotting bugs before I did, taking initiative without being asked, and defending decisions with data, I realised something had changed. We weren't just working for CouBon. We owned it. For student founders, especially, it's easy to misread what progress looks like. It's not just metrics. It's behaviour. If people are using your product on their own, if partners are finding you, and if your team is self-propelling, you're no longer just running a side project. You're running a company. These are what I now call "inflection indicators", not flashy, but quietly powerful. Because momentum doesn't just precede scale, it proves you're finally building something real.

Final Thoughts

By the end of May, CouBon had finally stabilised, but not in the way people often imagine startup success. There were no splashy headlines, no viral moments. What we had instead were habits. Students who came back week after week. Restaurant partners who no longer needed convincing. A team that had moved beyond hustle and into rhythm.

That kind of progress doesn't come with a trophy. But it comes with something far more useful: clarity.

The systems we had rebuilt, payment tracking, discount structures, and partner support, were no longer being tested in theory. They were being pressure-tested in real transactions, by real users, in real time. The numbers weren't massive, but they were honest. And more importantly, they were repeatable.

For the first time in months, I wasn't waking up to chaos. I was waking up to momentum.

But momentum, I quickly realised, is not the same as permanence. It's a window, and that window closes fast if you don't build scaffolding beneath it.

The very traction we had worked so hard to create now brought a different kind of tension: expectation. Could we take what worked in spring and make it last through fall? Could we grow without unravelling? Could we remain a tight, mission-driven team as responsibilities expanded and decisions became weightier?

And then there were the silent questions, the ones I didn't always speak aloud, even to my co-founders: Had we truly proven the model, or just bought ourselves time with well-placed discounts? Were we building something that could outgrow us, or something that only worked because we were pushing it day and night?

These weren't doubts. They were the kinds of questions that come not when you're losing, but when you've just started to win, and realise how much further there is to go.

Looking back, those late spring weeks didn't feel like a climax. They felt like the end of the prologue. We had proven we could build something real. Now came the harder part: proving it could last.

Most startups fear failure. But what I started to understand was this: early traction isn't the finish line, it's the starting gun. It's the moment people begin watching more closely, expecting more, and forgiving less. It's when your company stops being a scrappy idea and starts becoming a mirror of your systems, your discipline, and your leadership.

And so, as summer approached and most of the campus powered down, we didn't. We quietly geared up. Not for the next growth hack, pitch competition, or press feature. But for the foundational work that would determine whether CouBon could truly scale, or whether it was simply a semester-long experiment that had run its course.

Whatever the answer, one thing was clear: we wouldn't stumble into September. We'd be ready for it.

Chapter 7
The System Isn't Built for Student Founders. Build Anyway

As May approached, we had multiple goals in motion. We were past the initial launch and validation phase; this was about building smarter, growing sustainably, and preparing for the make-or-break moment that was the new year's student orientation season. Yet what became increasingly obvious was that while we were building a startup within the university ecosystem, the ecosystem wasn't built for us.

Building Smarter: Refining the Tech Stack

Rick and his team were heads down, improving the app based on the feedback we had accumulated over the previous weeks. One of the biggest friction points had been refunds. Up until then, every refund required us to manually e-transfer money to customers, a process that was clunky, slow, and, frankly, unprofessional. Rick built out an in-app credit system that changed the game. Now, once a refund request was approved, the user would instantly receive credit in their CouBon wallet, redeemable for future meals. It made the experience seamless and, importantly, gave us a powerful retention tool. Rather than issuing a cash outflow, we nudged users towards making another purchase, which benefited both restaurants and us, thanks to the commission structure.

Another feature that had long been requested by our restaurant partners was a tipping option. Previously, CouBon orders did not allow tipping, which, in a country like Canada, where tipping is customary and expected, felt like lost income to many restaurant staff. We implemented it, though with hesitation. Tipping is a deeply social act, often reinforced by the presence of a server. Our assumption was that digital orders would reduce the psychological pressure to tip, and we were right. Few users tipped through the app. But from the restaurant's perspective, we had acknowledged their concern and acted on it. That counted.

We also built a customisation feature for menu items, which allowed users to personalise their orders before checkout. Until then, restaurants would receive standard order emails that couldn't account for small preferences like "no onions" or "extra spicy." It was a minor backend change, but it made a big difference in operational accuracy and customer satisfaction.

Turning Data into Direction

On the data side, Meer and his team dove into user analytics. One of our biggest insights came from customer profiling. We categorised users into first-timers, return users, and "power users", those who used the app frequently and consistently. In May alone, we had one hundred and fifty new users. Seventy-seven used it at least twice, and seven people placed ten or more orders that month. One user even ordered seventeen times in the month.

These weren't just vanity stats. They proved we were starting to generate sticky demand, even without aggressive marketing and discount subsidies. It also told us that certain behaviours and usage patterns were worth doubling down on. If we could figure out what made someone a power user, we could engineer more of them.

One mistake early-stage founders make is dismissing their data because it feels too small to matter. But even limited usage can reveal actionable patterns, if you look closely. For us, seeing that certain users came back again and again helped us understand where the real value lay. It wasn't in flashy marketing; it was in reliability, convenience, and price. We didn't need thousands of data points to see that. Even with a handful of power users, we could reverse-engineer their behaviour and ask: How do we turn more people into them? For any student founder building without a massive budget, this kind of micro-analysis becomes your advantage. Big companies look for trends at scale. We could afford to look at people one by one.

This also extended to our restaurant partners. We identified our "power restaurants", those that brought in close to 1,000 orders in a single month. These partners weren't just profitable; they were predictable. For future restaurant acquisitions, we decided to focus on places that shared similar characteristics, cuisine type, price point, and proximity to students, increasing our odds of replicating success.

All this data helped us better prepare for orientation marketing. We now knew which restaurants resonated with students and which customer behaviours indicated long-term engagement. It turned guesswork into informed action.

Marketing Momentum and Misfires

Yashi and I had started laying the groundwork for our upcoming orientation campaigns. At this point, CouBon was relatively well-known among students, and this visibility opened unexpected doors. One such opportunity came from Science Rendezvous, a large University of Toronto fair that sees thousands of visitors annually. They invited us to sponsor part of the event, where we could facilitate our restaurant partners in setting up food stalls, selling through the CouBon app. It was a double win: we got more visibility, and our partners saw direct sales benefits.

We went all in. Ali coordinated with restaurant teams to ensure smooth operations, and Keita, our newly appointed third CFO, negotiated a favourable sponsorship deal. But this experience came with its own lesson. Because the event was largely organised by students, professionalism and accountability were inconsistent. Despite our prior agreement, there was a last-minute communication breakdown on their end, and we were almost dropped from the lineup. It took several panicked calls the day before the event to get things back on track.

That incident taught me a crucial founder lesson: when you're a student founder dealing with other students, expect things to go wrong. Assume miscommunication, double-confirm everything, and always have a backup plan.

Simultaneously, we were preparing to expand our restaurant network by targeting campuses beyond downtown Toronto. Keita, Ali, and I rented a car through a car-share app and visited suburban university neighbourhoods. We drove over 150 kilometres per day for three consecutive days, speaking with over a hundred restaurants during that time. This was partly a cost-optimisation decision. We wanted to minimise the number of rental days and maximise outreach.

But the reality we encountered was tough. Unlike downtown campuses, most suburban universities were isolated from their local restaurant ecosystems and had on-campus dining monopolies. When we pitched them on CouBon, the response was cold. "We already have a captive audience. Why offer discounts?" they argued. And from a business perspective, they weren't wrong. Still, we managed to convince a few reputable chains located near these campuses. Even if these weren't directly adjacent to the schools, they were known brands and could serve as beachheads.

Driving over 150 kilometres a day wasn't just physically draining; it was emotionally taxing in ways I hadn't anticipated. Every pitch started with optimism and ended, more often than not, with polite rejection or blank indifference. What wore me down wasn't the "no", it was the sheer volume of it; the realisation that even when our economics made perfect sense, people still clung to what was familiar. I remember walking into one popular franchise and being dismissed mid-sentence, the owner not even looking up from his phone. And yet, hours later, at a hole-in-the-wall shawarma joint, a tired but curious manager heard us out and signed on immediately. Moments like that kept us going. It reminded me that rejection, even when logical, isn't always final, and belief, when it does show up, often comes from the most unexpected places.

Institutional Resistance: The Silent Barrier

By August, the orientation season was fast approaching. This time, we weren't scrambling like the year before; we were deliberate. We retrained every restaurant's staff, ran mystery shopper tests, and ensured operational readiness across the board.

We also reached out to university campuses to be part of their official orientation activities. Some suburban campuses were open to the idea, but only if we agreed to upfront sponsorship. While we could technically afford it, I didn't want to deplete our limited capital so early. Instead, we offered to cater their events through our restaurant partners at a 20% discount. That way, restaurants generated volume-based revenue, which made them more loyal to us, and we got visibility, without handing out hard cash.

However, the response from our own campus was disheartening. Despite our traction and the fact that CouPon was a startup founded and run by its own students, we received no support. No promotional help. No official presence. Nothing. That institutional apathy stung. At the same time, our co-working space, which had been supporting us, suddenly asked for a significant rent increase. We tried negotiating. They wouldn't budge. We had to vacate the space.

I still remember sitting in that co-working space one last time: the walls bare, our whiteboard notes half-erased, trying to process how quickly support had turned into silence. Just weeks earlier, we were being applauded in mentorship meetings, encouraged to share our journey. Now, we were being priced out without a second thought. The rejection email from our own campus's orientation committee read like a formality, "due to policy, we regret...", but it hit harder than any VC pass. Not because we needed validation, but because we had earned the right to be seen. We weren't looking for handouts; we just wanted room to grow. That blow, more than anything, shifted my view of university entrepreneurship programs. The glossy posters, the startup showcases, the incubator invites – they often celebrated student founders only *after* someone else had backed them. Until then, we were just a risk buried in bureaucracy.

But we didn't slow down. Just like the year before, we showed up where we weren't invited, with confidence. We wore CouBon badges, carried printouts, and mingled like insiders. The orientation fairs were often back-to-back. From 11 a.m. to 5 p.m., we stood in the downtown sun promoting the app. Then we drove to suburban campuses and repeated the same grind from 7 p.m. to 10 p.m. The Canadian summer sun was relentless. It exhausted us more than winter ever had.

Our entire team was running on fumes. Almost everyone has fallen sick at least once. I lost my voice. But the student's response was incredible. Our download numbers nearly doubled. And while institutions ignored us, individuals didn't. Professors who knew our journey gave us shout-outs in lectures. Students we'd never met volunteered to help. That community made up for what the system denied.

The Campaigns That Didn't Click

Not everything we tried worked, and that's a lesson no founder escapes. One of our most anticipated early campaigns was at *Science Rendezvous*, a public-facing campus festival that we thought would be a golden opportunity. We had spent days planning our booth layout, printing QR flyers, and crafting a simple onboarding pitch: download CouBon, scan, and save. Thousands were expected to attend. It seemed like the perfect storm for a breakout moment.

What we didn't expect was an actual storm.

A steady drizzle turned into rain, and to make matters worse, a large-scale political protest broke out right next to the event venue. Roads were blocked, chants echoed across the street, and foot traffic, instead of being leisurely and curious, became fast-paced and distracted. Families, the main audience, hurried past with umbrellas, understandably uninterested in stopping for app demos. The few people who did engage often ended up paying in cash at the restaurant directly, bypassing the platform entirely. Despite all the preparation, CouBon barely registered. It was a washout in every sense.

The next stumble came during Orientation Week, where we launched a collaborative campaign with Tahini's, one of our popular restaurant partners. We designed an offer: students who placed an order through CouBon would receive a free glass of juice. The idea was to create a low-cost, high-engagement moment during a peak student activity week. But in execution, the process proved too complicated. Students had to download the app, navigate the interface, place an order, show a confirmation, and then claim the juice. Somewhere along that path, many got confused or simply gave up. The flow had too many steps. The drop-off was real.

Both campaigns fizzled quietly, and that quiet was painful. Not because of backlash, there was none, but because of the indifference. Silence doesn't offer feedback. It just leaves you wondering what went wrong.

Still, those misfires taught us something far more valuable than any textbook could. We learned that attention is not guaranteed; it's earned. If a campaign isn't intuitive within seconds, it likely won't convert. If the redemption flow isn't seamless, users will abandon it. And if your value proposition isn't instantly clear, it might as well not exist at all.

From that point on, we built a rule into every CouBon marketing discussion: if the average student can't understand and redeem the offer in under 10 seconds, it's too complicated. Simplicity became our north star. Because the truth is, in a crowded, distracted world, *if a user has to think twice, they won't act once.*

These failures didn't derail CouBon, but they did reshape it. They made us sharper, clearer, and more ruthless with friction. And in the long run, that clarity became one of our greatest assets.

Final Thoughts

Looking back, these months were some of the most defining in CouBon's journey, not because everything went to plan, but because we learned to thrive even when nothing did. We built smarter systems, dug deep into data, hustled across campuses, and doubled down on marketing. But more than anything, we learned how to endure.

We didn't grow because the system supported us; we grew because it didn't.

We lost resources, so we got resourceful. We were shut out of official platforms, so we built our own. We didn't have institutional allies, but we found champions in peers, professors, and restaurant owners who believed in what we were trying to do. The bureaucracy may have ignored us, but individuals showed up. And we made that count.

Being a student founder meant carrying double the load with half the privilege. It meant giving everything to a venture while still being expected to ace exams, secure internships, and act like you weren't building a business that fed hundreds of people every week. It meant being told *"you're too early"* by investors, *"you're too risky"* by administrators, and *"you're too ambitious"* by those who couldn't see the vision yet.

And still, we moved forward.

Because when no one expects you to win, even the smallest victory feels seismic. When the odds are stacked against you, you stop relying on the system and start becoming the system. That's the hidden strength of building as a student founder; there is no fallback, so your only direction is forward.

But even forward momentum has a cost. And as the dust settled post-orientation, I began to feel the weight of it all, not just in my schedule, but in my gut. It was a quiet, creeping question I hadn't yet allowed myself to answer: What happens when the fight begins to drain more than it builds?

Sometimes, the most important choice a founder makes isn't how to start. It's knowing when to stop, and why, that can still be a kind of victory.

After the rush of orientation faded, the weight of it all began to hit. Not just the fatigue, but the quiet mental clutter that builds up when you're juggling classes, partnerships, team morale, and institutional pushback all at once. My sleep suffered, my clarity dipped, and for the first time, I wasn't sure if the cost of pushing forward still matched the reward. It's something most student founders don't talk about enough: the burnout that doesn't come from doing too little, but from doing *everything*, constantly. We glorify hustle, but rarely ask: What are we actually sustaining? I had to start questioning whether continuing to push was still smart, or simply a habit. That's when I began to realise: letting go isn't always giving up. Sometimes, it's choosing to close the loop with intention, not exhaustion.

Chapter 8
When to Let Go (And Why That's Still Winning)

By October 2024, a heavy realisation had begun to dawn on me. The kind that creeps in gradually, then hits all at once.

If CouBon was going to become a sustainable business, one that could pay even a modest living wage to the core team, we would need to scale to a level that felt increasingly out of reach. At the time, our gross profit per transaction was just under $1. If we wanted to pay four team members even a modest $40,000 per year, plus another $40,000 for operational expenses, we'd need over 200,000 transactions annually just to break even. That wasn't including marketing spend, legal costs, or any form of founder upside. And we were nowhere close to that figure. Our projected annual volume was in the low thousands.

This wasn't a minor gap; it was a chasm.

Inflation, Tariffs, and a Crumbling Business Case

It wasn't just our internal numbers painting a grim picture. Conversations with restaurant owners were revealing new pressures. One of our long-time cafe partners shared that coffee bean prices had jumped by 30% in just six months. Another, running a small fast-food outlet, told us meat prices had nearly doubled since last year. Canada's food inflation wasn't just theoretical; it was pounding the unit economics of local restaurants.

Add to this the growing uncertainty around U.S.-Canada trade tariffs and a weakening CAD, and the outlook becomes even more concerning. Many ingredients, especially those used in international cuisines, were imported. A weaker dollar meant higher ingredient costs. But restaurants couldn't just hike prices to compensate. Domestic incomes were stagnant, and with recession clouds gathering, customers were becoming even more price-sensitive.

The result? Our partners were being squeezed from both ends. Their costs were rising, their margins shrinking, and the last thing they wanted was to layer on steep discounts through CouBon. We started seeing this play out directly: new restaurant acquisitions became harder. The discounts we once easily negotiated were now met with hesitation or outright rejection.

This created a painful dilemma. CouBon was built on the promise of helping students eat affordably, students like us, juggling tuition, rent, and groceries. But the very restaurants that enabled that mission were now struggling to survive. Asking them for deeper discounts started to feel exploitative, even if unintentional. I found myself on calls with owners who genuinely liked what we were doing, but who couldn't justify giving 20% off when their food costs had ballooned. And I didn't blame them. For the first time, it felt like we were stuck between two sides of the same economic crisis, trying to serve both, and disappointing both. That moral discomfort only added to the growing sense that our model might not fit the moment anymore.

What made our platform attractive, helping fill off-peak hours through discounts, was becoming less relevant in an economy where every hour was becoming a fight for survival.

Two Roads: One Funding Round or a Final Chapter

Faced with this, we had to choose between two difficult paths.

Option one: raise another round, this time, significantly larger than before. A five-digit cheque wouldn't cut it. We needed six figures. Enough to grow marketing, support operations, and maybe even offer part-time stipends to keep core members around.

Option two: wind it down.

None of us wanted the second option. Not yet. CouBon had become more than a company to us. So we chose to try one more push. We crafted updated decks, sharpened our metrics, and reached out to investors, VCs, large angels, and senior operators. Some showed interest. We progressed through initial calls and second rounds. But by the third call, the answer was nearly always the same: a polite but firm no.

Some investors were candid. They didn't like the restaurant space. Others were spooked by the macroeconomics. A few simply didn't believe the model could scale. We weren't just trying to prove CouBon, we were fighting a tide of scepticism towards consumer food-tech businesses.

Still, we didn't give up. We had a few promising calls with major angels, one was the Head of AI at a global firm based in the U.S., and another was an F&B conglomerate founder. We held on, hoping one "yes" could shift our momentum.

But even hope, when stretched too long, begins to thin.

The Call That Changed Everything

While we were chasing investor calls, something else was unravelling quietly, our team. Some of our earliest contributors were now focused on job applications and grad school. Response times lengthened. Ownership dipped. No one wanted to admit it, but I could tell: people had mentally checked out.

One Wednesday night, I called Rick.

I had rehearsed what I wanted to say, but even then, it felt like jumping off a cliff. I told him I'd been thinking about the big picture, our growth rate, the market shifts, the fundraising fatigue, and that maybe it was time to consider letting go.

There was a long pause on the line. Then Rick broke down. And in that moment, I did too.

It wasn't just a startup. It was our identity. For the past two years, CouBon had been my purpose, my obsession, my answer to every *"what are you working on?"* question. My friends asked about CouBon before they asked how I was doing. It was inseparable from who I had become.

For me, CouBon wasn't just a startup; it was a shield. It gave me a sense of direction, purpose, and even social currency. When people introduced me, it was always *"he's the founder of CouBon."* That label had become such a defining part of my identity that the thought of losing it felt like losing my place in the world. Would people still take me seriously without it? Would I even take *myself* seriously? I had built my self-worth around traction, investor calls, and onboarding wins. Without those, I feared becoming invisible. The morning after that call with Rick, everything felt quieter, but not in a peaceful way. My phone wasn't buzzing. Slack wasn't active. And in that silence, I heard something I hadn't heard in months: doubt. Not about CouBon, but about myself. Who was I if not this?

Now I was wondering what life would look like without it.

What would I tell my parents, who had supported me so fiercely? What would investors think if I had wasted their trust? What would it mean for the goals I had set, the dream of proving that a student founder could build something meaningful, credible, and long-lasting?

Rick and I decided to give it ten more days. One last deep dive. No decisions made in grief or exhaustion.

The Conference Room

The next day, I spoke to Meer and Ali, who were now what remained of our core team. I kept it quiet, but they could tell something had shifted. Over the next ten days, I barely slept. I ran through every KPI, every trend line. Meer and I had long, late-night calls dissecting data, forecasting scenarios, and imagining pivots. But every scenario, no matter how creative, pointed to the same conclusion: we were trying to build against the wind.

Ten days later, Rick, Ali, and I gathered in the conference room, one that had seen countless meetings, brainstorms, and product discussions. This one felt different. There was no whiteboard. No agenda. Just quiet understanding.

We talked, not like co-founders, but like friends who had been through something life-changing together. At one point, I closed my laptop and said what we were all thinking: "We could keep pushing for another three months, but we know what that would look like." Everyone nodded. There was no dramatic tension, no emotional outbursts. Just a shared understanding that continuing would mean fighting inertia with no real change in trajectory. We had exhausted every lever, marketing campaigns, pricing models, outreach pushes, and while there were still small wins, we weren't moving towards something greater anymore. We were looping.

Then came the part I'll never forget.

We made the decision to shut it down unanimously. No one had to be convinced. And for me, that moment mattered more than I can explain. It wasn't just a decision; it was *ours*. CouBon had started as my idea, but in that conference room, it became clear that it belonged to all of us. That shared ownership, especially at the end, was one of the most meaningful things I'd experienced as a founder. It wasn't just a company we had built together; it was a journey we had co-authored.

After we closed our laptops and packed our things, Ali left first. He had class and gave us both a nod before heading out. But Rick and I stayed behind, sitting in silence for a few extra minutes, not saying much, just letting it all sink in.

Before we finally stood up, Rick looked at me and said, "I know we'll all achieve something great in the future. This is just the start." I didn't say much back, just smiled. But I held onto those words. Because in that moment, they felt less like comfort and more like conviction.

Walking out of that room wasn't easy. But it wasn't bitter either. We hadn't failed because we were lazy or misguided. We had just reached the natural limit of what CouBon could be. And sometimes, knowing when to let go is the most mature decision a founder can make, not because you've given up, but because you know more time won't change the outcome. We had done the work. We had taken every shot. And now, it was time to make space for what would come next.

That conference room didn't just mark the end of CouBon; it marked the beginning of closure. And as I walked out, I wasn't walking away from something; I was walking forward, with everything it had taught me.

Shutting Down the Right Way

Once we made the decision in that conference room, I knew I couldn't let it linger. When a startup dies slowly, it hurts more: for the team, for the users, for the founder who keeps clinging to what was. So I chose to act swiftly, out of respect for everything CouBon had been, and everyone who had believed in it.

The first step was the hardest: informing our investors. I spent the next 48 hours setting up back-to-back calls. No email blasts. No vague summaries. Just one-on-one conversations with the people who had taken a bet on us, many when we were nothing more than two students with a deck and a dream.

I didn't dress up the story. I didn't talk about "strategic pivots" or use words like "pause" or "restructure." I told them the truth: that we had tried everything we could, that we were proud of what we had built, and that the time had come to close this chapter.

What happened next caught me off guard.

Not a single investor pushed back. Not one asked for justifications or post-mortems. Instead, I heard phrases like, *"This is the most transparent wind-down*

I've seen." "You earned our respect." And most importantly, *"Whatever you build next, please keep me in the loop."*

Those words mattered more than I can describe. Because in those moments, I was still wrestling with the loudest voice in the room: my own. The voice that whispered failure. That replayed all the things we could've done differently. That measured my worth against CouBon's outcome. But hearing those votes of confidence, especially from people who had skin in the game, reminded me that integrity travels further than success alone.

It was a kind of closure money couldn't buy.

On December 31st, 2024, CouBon officially ceased operations. The symbolism of ending on the last day of the year wasn't lost on me. A full circle. A clean ending. I drafted our final announcement for social media with a knot in my stomach, not because I regretted anything, but because I knew how much the journey had meant to me.

We didn't post it with fanfare or PR polish. Just a short message of gratitude, reflection, and acknowledgement of the people who had made it all possible.

And then something unexpected happened.

Messages poured in. Dozens at first, then hundreds. From close friends, sure, but also from strangers. Students who said CouBon helped them eat better during tight months. New founders who said they had followed our journey and found courage through it. Alumni who remembered our early Instagram stories and said, *"You made campus life more vibrant."*

Student clubs began reposting the announcement, adding their own captions about what CouBon meant to them. Some thanked us for being part of their event memories. Others simply wrote, *"You did something brave."*

For the first time in weeks, I felt less alone.

Because the hardest part about shutting something down isn't logistics, it's emotional. It's the silence that comes after. The calendar slots that no longer exist. The Slack pings that don't arrive. The team syncs that disappear. It's the realisation that something that once demanded your every breath now exists only in memory.

But what the messages showed me was this: CouBon hadn't disappeared. It had imprinted. On people. On the ecosystem. On me.

It didn't end in fireworks or headlines, but it ended with dignity. And that, I've come to believe, is a kind of success too.

Aftermath and the Quarter-Life Crisis

Still, nothing prepares you for the emotional vacuum of winding down your startup, especially when it's become your identity.

For weeks after we closed, I went silent. I didn't post. I didn't pitch. I didn't plan. On my 21st birthday in late December, I found myself staring at the ceiling and wondering: what now?

That was my quarter-life crisis. And it was real. The high-octane rhythm of startup life had vanished. No meetings. No dashboards. No late-night Slack messages. Just stillness.

But slowly, clarity began to form.

I realised that while CouBon had ended, my journey as a founder hadn't. I still wanted to be an entrepreneur. I just had to approach it differently.

Designing a 5-Year Recovery Plan

I sat down with a blank sheet of paper and asked myself: If I wanted to be a successful founder five years from now, what would I need?

Three pillars emerged: subject knowledge, network, and personal brand.

Subject knowledge: I needed deep insight into an industry worth building in. Not a passing interest, but an edge.

Network: I needed to surround myself with the kind of people who could be co-founders, backers, advisors, not just acquaintances.

Personal brand: I needed credibility, something that said, "I've done the work."

Through multiple conversations with VCs, I had noticed where they were investing: cleantech, fintech, and healthtech. Sectors with tailwinds, systemic impact, and defensible models.

I decided then that I would dedicate the next few years to equipping myself in these facets to be better positioned to succeed in the future.

So in January, I joined Xatoms, a Forbes 30 Under 30 cleantech startup using machine learning to create light-sensitive particles for water purification. I wanted to understand what it looked like to build a venture at the cutting edge, one that solved problems at scale and depth. It gave me structure. It gave me curiosity again.

What surprised me most was how different the energy felt. At Xatoms, the problems were harder, more technical, and far less glamorous, but the focus was razor-sharp. There was no performative hustle, no obsession with going viral. Just scientists and engineers working relentlessly on a real-world problem. I found it grounding. There were meetings where I didn't understand half the science being discussed, but instead of feeling out of place, I felt inspired. This was a different kind of entrepreneurship, one rooted in depth over speed. And slowly, that started to heal something in me. I realised I didn't need to always be the most visible or the one in charge to feel valuable. Sometimes, learning quietly was its own kind of progress.

One detail that stuck with me was how seriously the team approached even small university pitch competitions. I remember them preparing with full decks and rehearsals for events where the prize money was as little as $100. At first, I didn't get it. They weren't in it for the cash. But over time, I realised what they were really chasing: credibility. Each minor win added to their story, another notch that made the next grant, the next accelerator, the next publication more plausible. That accumulation of recognition, no matter how small each piece looked on its own, was what helped propel them towards meaningful acclaim, including their eventual Forbes 30 Under 30 nod.

It made me reflect on my own choices with CouBon. I had been so focused on building, on solving operational challenges, scaling, and making the business work that I only pursued pitch competitions where the prize money justified the time investment. If it wasn't a few thousand dollars, I didn't see the point. But maybe I'd missed something. Maybe the act of showing up, telling your story, and collecting small external validations mattered more than I had realised, not for ego, but for momentum. At Xatoms, I saw that those early signals of seriousness could shape perception. And perception, in the startup world, often precedes traction.

Xatoms reminded me that credibility isn't always built in leaps. Sometimes, it's stitched together from small wins, each one amplifying the next. And in those quiet moments, watching a team of scientists treat $100 competitions with the same respect as $1 million grants, I understood the long game differently.

That lesson stayed with me, not just as a tactical insight, but as a shift in mindset. I had spent so much time at CouBon focused on outcomes that I often overlooked the value of visibility along the way. Xatoms reminded me that sometimes, the quiet ones matter just as much as the loud ones. And more importantly, that rebuilding doesn't always mean rushing into the next idea; it can start with observing, absorbing, and recalibrating.

The reason I share this is that every student founder who closes their first venture will feel that void. It's unavoidable. But how you fill that void matters. You can spiral, or you can strategise. I chose the latter.

What Closure Taught Me Is That Success Never Could

In the months since CouBon's closure, I've come to appreciate that its most lasting lessons weren't in the highs, but in how we chose to handle the ending.

Over the course of two years, I had lived through the full spectrum of the founder journey: forming a team, building a product, launching, pivoting, fundraising, scaling, stumbling, and ultimately deciding to shut it all down. It was, in every sense, a real-world MBA, condensed, unsparing, and earned. But more than skillsets, it left me with something far rarer: clarity.

CouBon taught me that being a founder isn't about charisma, visibility, or even perseverance alone. It's about discipline, the ability to make decisions that serve the company, not your ego. It's about knowing when to fight harder and when to walk away with your principles intact. The act of letting go, done deliberately and transparently, was the clearest expression of that maturity. We didn't close because we failed. We closed because we knew the cost of continuing outweighed the reward. That takes courage. And that courage, I've come to realise, is a form of success in itself.

What I carry forward isn't just what worked, but what we were brave enough to walk away from when it didn't.

Final Thoughts

Letting go of CouBon didn't subtract from the story; it sharpened it. It cleared space for a more grounded version of myself to emerge. One less attached to optics, and more committed to substance.

We often romanticise resilience as synonymous with endurance: keep going, push harder, never quit. But there's a quieter form of resilience that gets far less attention, the kind that requires stepping back, reflecting deeply, and acknowledging when continuing isn't courage, but avoidance. That kind of resilience doesn't make headlines. But it builds character. And that's what CouBon gave me, more than anything else, a hard-won clarity of self.

I no longer look at success in binaries. I don't see endings as losses or pivots as failures. I see them as signals. The truth is, building something that matters takes more than just passion or grit; it takes alignment. Between your vision and the market. Between your values and your choices. Between what you're building and who you're becoming in the process.

CouBon taught me to ask better questions. Not just, *is this working?* But *is this still worth it?* Not just, *can we keep going?* But *should we?* Those aren't questions you can Google or outsource. They come from brutal honesty with yourself, and they're the ones that define your trajectory far more than any vanity metric ever could.

It also made me confront what I had been avoiding: that I had wrapped so much of my identity in the role of "founder" that I forgot I was allowed to exist outside of it. The quiet that followed CouBon's closure forced me to separate my self-worth from my startup's worth. That process wasn't comfortable, but it was necessary. Because if your confidence depends entirely on your current title, it was never truly confidence to begin with.

And here's what surprised me most: once the noise faded, what remained was stronger than I expected. A deeper understanding of how I want to lead. A sharper sense of what kind of problems I want to solve. A new reverence for sustainability, not just in business models, but in pace, partnerships, and purpose.

CouBon gave me a front-row seat to what it means to build. But its ending taught me what it means to evolve.

So if you're someone at the start of your journey, or someone quietly questioning whether it's time to end one, I hope you know this: you're not less of a founder because you chose to let go. You might just be more of one.

Because in the end, it's not the size of the outcome that defines you. It's the integrity of your choices, the honesty of your process, and the depth of what you carry forward. CouBon may no longer exist as a product, but as a proving ground, as a teacher, and as a mirror, its impact is still unfolding in me.

And in ways I didn't expect, it gave me something better than confidence; it gave me conviction.

Conclusion
What I'd Tell the 18-Year-Old Me

If I could sit across from my 18-year-old self, the one who had just scribbled CouBon's first idea in a notebook, I wouldn't offer advice in bullet points. I wouldn't tell him how to raise capital or write better cold emails. I'd tell him something simpler, something deeper:

You have no idea what's about to happen. And that's a gift.

Because this path won't unfold like a business plan, it'll unfold like a mirror, showing you everything you didn't know about yourself, and everything you didn't know you were strong enough to survive. You'll think you're building a startup. But really, you're building a founder.

Over the last two years, I've lived the full arc: idea, execution, growth, loss, and ultimately, closure. And through that journey, five lessons became anchors for me. They're what I wish someone had whispered in my ear before I started. So here they are now, offered to the version of me that didn't yet know how hard it would get, and to anyone just now stepping into the arena.

1. **Start Before You're Ready**

    You will never feel ready. Not for your first pitch, not for your first launch, not even for your first "yes." Starting a company while still a student will feel audacious, because it is. You'll doubt whether your idea is solid enough, whether your skill set is sharp enough, and whether your timing is right. And the truth is: it probably isn't. But if you wait until it is, you'll never begin.

    When we started CouBon, we didn't have institutional backing. We didn't have a polished product or a roadmap for growth. What we had was urgency. A sense that the idea deserved action, even if we weren't sure how to pull it off. That urgency turned into movement. And that movement turned into learning. Start before you're ready, and let the doing teach you what the planning never could.

The first version of your product will probably be flawed. Your pitch will be rough. Your assumptions will be wrong. That's not a sign to stop, it's a signal to iterate. Readiness is rarely a prerequisite for impact. But commitment? That's essential.

2. **Build for Truth, Not Just for Traction**

    Traction feels incredible. Investor interest, user growth, and media attention create a rush. But they can also distort reality. It's easy to start measuring your progress based on how good the numbers look in a pitch deck, rather than how sound the business truly is.

There were moments in CouBon where we felt the high. Our downloads were growing. We were onboarding new restaurants. From the outside, we looked like a student-run rocket ship. But internally, I had a growing unease. Our gross profit per order was thin. Our model depended on discounts that restaurants were growing hesitant to give. Our projected transaction volume wasn't close to what we needed to break even, let alone pay ourselves a fair wage.

And yet, we pushed. We polished decks, we quoted stats that looked good out of context, we leaned on the narrative. That wasn't deceit, it was hope. But hope isn't a strategy. I realised too late that every time I postponed a hard conversation, for fear of slowing momentum, I was trading long-term stability for short-term appearances.

Founders often hear *"fake it till you make it."* But sometimes, that mantra just delays necessary decisions. You can't pivot from a myth. You can only pivot from the truth.

So build for truth. Ask the uncomfortable questions. Audit your economics before your ego: whether it is your business model or the industry you seek to operate in. The longer you delay reality, the steeper the cost when it catches up.

3. **No One Will Give You Permission, Own It Anyway**

    As a student founder, you'll often feel like an outsider. You won't have the alumni network, the MBA credibility, or the polished narrative. Institutions may celebrate student entrepreneurship in theory, but in practice, they rarely offer meaningful support until you're already "proven."

At CouBon, we faced this over and over. Our own campus denied us access to orientation events. Co-working spaces increased our rent overnight. Startups that had no revenue and no traction were being propped up by accelerators, while we, who had users, partners, and profit, were constantly told "not yet."

You cannot wait for validation. You cannot rely on gatekeepers to recognise your legitimacy. If you walk into a room like you belong, half the time, people will believe you do. The other half, you'll need to prove it. Either way, don't apologise for building early. Don't shrink because your email signature doesn't end in a degree or title. You're not an amateur. You're just early.

Founders don't ask for permission. They assume responsibility.

4. Closing Isn't Quitting. It's Leading.

No one talks about what it means to shut down your first company. And when you're in the middle of it, it feels like grief, because it is. You've poured yourself into something, made it your identity, sacrificed sleep, stability, and in some cases, sanity. And now you're deciding to step away. You worry about what people will say. You fear what silence will feel like when the Slack channel goes dark.

But I'll tell you what I learned: the hardest part isn't telling the world, it's telling yourself.

When we made the decision to close CouBon, I thought I'd feel like a failure. But the moment we made it official, I felt something else: clarity. We hadn't made that decision lightly. We had reviewed the numbers, the market conditions, and the team dynamics. And most of all, we had decided not to lie to our investors, to our customers, or to ourselves.

There's strength in that.

Leadership isn't about clinging on until the wheels fall off. It's about knowing when the road ahead isn't worth the fuel. It's about closing loops with honesty and showing your team what integrity looks like in real time. Walking away isn't weak. It's wisdom.

5. **You're Building a Founder, Not Just a Startup**
   This is the most important lesson of all. Everything you're going through: every win, every setback, every moment of doubt, is shaping not just the business, but you.

The skills you're developing, resourcefulness, resilience, communication, and empathy, will outlast the company. You're learning how to take risks, build systems, make decisions under uncertainty, and live with the consequences. That's the real startup. That's the real product.

CouBon didn't survive. But I did. And in doing so, I became someone more capable of building what comes next.

So measure your growth not just in users or revenue, but in perspective. Ask yourself: Am I becoming sharper? More honest? More grounded? Because your next idea will be better. And when it comes, you'll be ready to lead it, not just launch it.

Why Failure Isn't the Opposite of Success

Let's be clear: failure hurts. It stings when people stop asking about your startup. It feels isolating when you go from being "the founder" to someone who "used to run that thing." There's a quiet shame, especially when you poured everything into it.

But failure, when done right, is not the end. It's a phase of becoming. And it comes with dividends no one sees at first: deeper self-awareness, sharper instincts, and a kind of humility that strengthens conviction, not weakens it.

Every successful founder you admire has failed at something before. Most won't even tell you the full story. But it's there in the background. In the way they negotiate better, listen more, raise smarter, or build more defensible products.

Failure, done openly and honestly, is an education that no classroom can match.

Failure also redefined how I relate to others. I became a better listener, more empathetic to those building things that weren't quite working, because I had lived through that quiet panic. I now see the early stages of startups not just with excitement, but with caution. I've sat on the other side of the table knowing how much is at stake for a founder emotionally, not just financially.

It also made me more intentional. I no longer chase opportunities just because they look good on paper. I vet for alignment, mission, and long-term durability. I ask harder questions before I say yes because I've seen what happens when passion runs ahead of structure.

But most importantly, failure taught me how to reset without resentment. I could've spent months replaying what went wrong. But instead, I used those lessons as raw material for what came next. It made me hungrier, but also calmer. More ambitious, but less anxious. It gave me a more grounded kind of confidence, the kind that doesn't need external proof.

I wouldn't trade that kind of clarity for anything.

So, if you're navigating failure, don't just survive it. Study it. Let it humble you, sharpen you, and soften you at the same time. There's a quieter form of success hidden inside it, the kind that no one applauds, but that changes everything.

To Those Still Unsure, Still Scared, Still Starting

If you're just getting started, here's what I want you to know: it's okay to feel unsure. It's okay to be overwhelmed. It's okay to wonder whether you're cut out for this, whatever *this* looks like for you.

Entrepreneurship rarely feels like the confident highlight reel we're fed. It's a series of stumbles, guesses, and half-built ideas held together by nothing but belief. And even that belief will waver. Mine did, more than once.

But if the pull to build something of your own is real, even if it's faint, honour it. You don't need to have it all figured out. You don't need a perfect pitch deck, a viral launch, or a roadmap that impresses investors. You just need a reason that matters to you, and the willingness to chase it one imperfect step at a time.

There will be days when no one claps for you. Keep showing up anyway.

There will be moments when the people closest to you don't understand your vision. Hold it anyway.

There may come a point, like it did for me, when you're forced to ask whether continuing is still worth it. And if the answer is no, walk away with your head high. Closing something down doesn't make you less of a founder. It makes you the kind of founder who can be trusted to lead again.

This journey isn't linear. It's rarely glamorous. You'll second-guess yourself more times than you'll celebrate. But the fact that you're even entertaining the idea of starting puts you ahead of most because starting requires something that no degree, no title, no resume can give you: the willingness to be seen trying.

So if you're scared, start anyway. If you're not ready, start anyway. Just begin, quietly, messily, without fanfare.

And when you inevitably fall, don't let it define you. Let it refine you.

Because no matter how long it takes, no matter how many times you have to rebuild from scratch, the fact that you care this much about solving something, building something, becoming something, is already proof that you're someone worth betting on.